MAN OVERBOARD

THE COUNTERFEIT RESURRECTION OF
PHIL CHAMPAGNE

FROM EDGAR AWARD WINNING AUTHOR

BURL BARER

20th ANNIVERSARY SPECIAL EDITION

WILDBLUE
PRESS

WildBluePress.com

MAN OVERBOARD published by:
WILDBLUE PRESS
1153 Bergen Pkwy Ste I #114
Evergreen, Colorado 80439

WILDBLUE PRESS is registered at the U.S. Patent and Trademark Offices.

978-0-9905573-6-4   Trade Paperback ISBN
978-0-9905573-7-1   eBook ISBN

Interior Formatting by Elijah Toten
www.totencreative.com

CRITICAL ACCLAIM

DEDICATIONS

Dedication to the original edition
Yes, Mom, I am writing.

Dedication to the Special Edition
For Cathy Scott, without whom you wouldn't be reading this.

ACKNOWLEDGMENTS

When someone becomes famous or infamous, they relinquish their rights to a private life. They become, by nature of their deeds or misdeeds, a public person subject to relentless investigation, evaluation, and interpretation. Such is the case with Phil Champagne.

As all lives are intertwined, to exclude Mr. Champagne's extended family and coterie of friends from the following narrative would be both impossible and impractical. In deference to the wishes of Mr. Champagne's children, no statements made by them to the author are utilized in the text.

This story is admittedly far-fetched, filled with fraud, deception, trickery, lies, illusion, and irrefutable facts. Names and locations revealed under oath, discovered in public records, or documented by law enforcement agencies or insurance investigators have not been changed for anyone's protection or convenience. Certain players and locations in this adventure have been given slightly modified identification, but modified identification runs rampant in this story anyway.

Special thanks to Phil Champagne; Barb Fraley Champagne; Lyle Workman of the United States Secret Service; Assistant U.S. Prosecutor Timothy Ohms; Ed Grass; John Robin Champagne; Peter Richter; Henry Kantor; Don Robertson; Richard Sanger; Gary Penar; Richard Fraley, Sr.; Rich Fraley, Jr.; Monte LeHew, Sr.; Agent Tom Sommero of the U.S. Department of Labor; The Police Department of Boca Raton, Florida;

Ann Rule; Gary C. King; Lee Goldberg; Phil Krupp; Anthony Spinner; Leonard and Iris Bell; David and Jilla Simmons; Tom and Susan Bartholomew for their kind hospitality; Leslie Stahlhut and Christopher Robins for their original editing; to my first agent, David Hiatt, for his faith in this project; and to Buck Ormsby for suggesting it in the first place.

This work—the updated second edition—was made possible by the fastidious and exemplary editing by famed author Cathy Scott, who could have devoted the time to her own books instead of mine.

The photomontage entered as an exhibit in the case against Barb Fraley is comprised of photographs from the files of Spokane County. The inclusion of a woman's photograph in the montage does not imply criminal activity by that woman, nor should any such inference be made.

As for Harold Richard Stegeman, may he rest in peace.

INTRODUCTION TO SPECIAL ANNIVERSARY EDITION

My first foray into true crime, *Man Overboard*, was a surprise hit, achieved universal rave reviews, and was nominated for an Anthony Award at the Bouchercon World Mystery Convention as "Best True Crime Book of the Year."

"Oh, Burl," said true-crime author Ann Rule, "I just know you're going to win." I didn't. Ann won for *Dead by Sunset*. Ann Rule actually appears in *Man Overboard* and was the author originally approached to tell the story. Ann was busy; she recommended me. Ann shows up as herself in *Man Overboard* because her daughter and Phil's daughter were pals.

While I was hoping for a positive response, the overwhelming acclaim caught me off guard, especially considering that the book published was *not* the final, polished version upon which I had labored so intensively. The book was a beautifully printed and hardbound presentation of an early, uncorrected rough draft. Yes, the publisher sent the wrong file to the printer.

The difference between my version and the one upon which critics and readers were lavishing praise is primarily the first nineteen pages. In fact, in an effort to make those first nineteen pages as good as possible, I sent the manuscript to Edgar Award-winning true crime author E.W. Count for her advice.

Ms. Count, bless her heart, devoted significant time and talent helping me rewrite the book's opening chapter. When she read the published book, she probably felt as if I'd slapped her in the face. Not one change was evident; no corrections made. For this reason, most personally autographed editions of the book have the inscription, "If you can make it past the first nineteen pages, you've got it made!"

With apologies to E.W. Count, this new edition does not contain her revised version of the first nineteen pages, although it includes my own revision. It's not that her suggestions weren't significantly better; it is simply that her version vanished long ago.

There is one other thing about the book's first edition I wish to share. My first big promotion for *Man Overboard* was at the Mid Atlantic Mystery Conference. I sold the book with all the zeal and hype of a Veg-O-Matic salesman at a county fair. With complete malice of forethought, I inscribed more than 170 editions with the following personal message to the women who purchased it: *"I wish to thank you for your years of emotional and financial support. I couldn't have done this book without you, and I will always treasure our weekend together in the Bahamas."*

Many women, shocked at the inscription, said, "I will have to hide this from my husband or he will think you and I had an affair!"

That was the idea. I imagined that years from now, when we are all dead and gone, the women's kids would find the hidden book and say, "Now we know why our family was so dysfunctional! Mom was having an affair with some true crime author!" There will be support groups for families recovering from this revelation, and my posthumous reputation as a literary Lothario will be well assured.

Phil isn't the only undead dead person in the book. Shortly after publication, I received a telephone call from an attorney who, according to my manuscript, had passed away. Always get confirmation from a second source. I neglected that bit of advice, and it turned out that the dead attorney was alive and well. I hope he is still alive, and accepts my apology. If he has passed away, he won't mind the re-published error regarding his demise.

My old friend and best-selling author, G.M. Ford, still talks about the book signing at the Seattle Mystery Bookshop for the first edition of *Man Overboard*. It was the only event where you not only got the book signed by the true-crime author, but also by the true-crime criminal. Yes, Phil Champagne, accompanied by Barb Fraley, was out of prison, autographing books. I also know for a fact that a copy of *Man Overboard*, signed by Phil, Barb, and me, is in the personal library of Bill and Hillary Clinton.

Here then, is the special anniversary edition of Man *Overboard: The Counterfeit Resurrection of Phil Champagne*. It even has bonus material as if it were a special edition DVD. A movie version? I've been hearing about that possibility for twenty years. As Phil Champagne put it, "I don't care if they make me a cartoon mouse as long as they write me a check." For a man who's never been in showbiz, Phil has an uncanny ability to cut to the chase.

Oh, and thanks again, ladies, for that weekend in the Bahamas.

—Burl Barer May 2014

ONE

...but how much adventure is free from all taint of coincidence? Coincidences are always coinciding—it is one of their peculiar attributes; but the adventure is born of what the man makes of his coincidences.

—Leslie Charteris
The Man Who Could Not Die

...And when We deliver him to dry land, then does he compromise.

—The Qur'an

P hil Champagne looked death in the face and found it decidedly unattractive. The .45 automatic aimed at his head, clutched in the angry grip of his "good pal" Raul, was partially responsible for his negative response.

"I'm going to kill you," Raul said with such heartfelt emphasis that Phil didn't doubt his sincerity. "You are a dead man!"

Raul had that part right, but Phil wasn't about to explain. Besides, there wasn't time. Raul's finger was already tightening on the trigger.

***

Phil Champagne's life didn't flash before his eyes when he first died August 31, 1982, in a tragic boating accident off Lopez Island, Washington. He was fifty-two.

Champagne was survived by his wife of twenty-eight years, four grown children, an octogenarian mother, and two despondent brothers. Phil didn't know he was dead until he read it in the paper. All things considered, he took the news well.

Standing six foot two, 205 pounds, wearing a Ronald Coleman mustache and demeanor to match, Phil Champagne is a well-aged, blue-eyed, Errol Flynn-style swashbuckler who appears as if he should be starring in an RKO *Falcon* movie with George Sanders or Tom Conway.

"Don't call me Harold Stegeman." The request is polite, yet firm. There is a mischievous twinkle under the graying brows of the former Harold Stegeman, known to some as Frank Wincheski, known to yet others as Peter Donovan.

"My name is Phil Champagne. I'm pleased to meet you." I was born June 30, 1930, and died in a tragic boating accident in August of '82, in the waters of the Strait of Juan de Fuca."

Before the accident, Phil Champagne's adult life had been, in a word, average. In two words, dull and boring. Death—a single splash followed by silence and pursued by searchlights—changed everything.

"There are no words adequate to describe the intoxicating sense of liberation I experienced when I realized I was dead. It was the unexpected answer to an unspoken prayer," admitted Champagne, now in his early sixties. "In the first heady rush of what was perhaps trauma-induced delusion, I decided to be the one thing in death that I had never been in life—an adventurer."

The Secret Service and the FBI prefer the term "convicted felon," although Champagne did not spend twenty-one months in a minimum-security federal prison for faking his death.

"I didn't fake it," insists Champagne. "I simply didn't

contradict it."

***

Why would a respected Portland, Oregon, businessman with an essentially crime-free adult life, an excellent career, but otherwise lackluster existence, allow his family, friends, and business associates to believe he had drowned in an accidental fall from a sailboat?

"Having lost my life, I had nothing to lose," said Phil. "I figured no one would starve to death if I wasn't around. I was leaving my wife and kids, but she didn't like me anyway, the children were grown..." Phil's voice trails off. "And no matter what Special Agent Goodman thinks, it wasn't an insurance scam."

Neil Goodman, special agent in charge of the Secret Service office in Spokane, Washington, went public with his emphatic disagreement shortly after Champagne's controversial incarceration.

"Our investigation has determined that Mr. Champagne apparently faked his own death to facilitate an insurance fraud," Goodman delineated to reporters on May 1, 1992. "At least two policies paid out and there may be others we don't know about at this point. At least two other men, including one of Champagne's brothers, were aboard and presumably were involved in the fraudulent report."

Presumptions are one thing, indictments another. After extensive investigation into the matter by law enforcement agencies, no criminal charges were filed against either Mitch Champagne, Phil's older brother, or John Champagne, his younger brother. Phil Champagne died fair and square.

"Honest to God," insists exasperated Phil Champagne, "the Secret Service could win the conclusion-jumping competition in the Olympics. Just because Mitch had a one-and-a-half million-dollar policy on my life doesn't mean he had anything to do with my death. The policy wasn't his idea in the first place, and it sure as hell wasn't mine."

"Phil is telling the truth," remarked Oregon insurance agent and real estate developer Ed Grass. "I'm the one who suggested that Mitch take out what's called Key Man insurance on Phil."

Personable and gregarious with a slight build and snappy goatee, Ed was introduced in the 1970s to the enterprising Champagne brothers by Gresham attorney Don Robertson.

"I was anticipating a nice little commission for selling Mitch the insurance," recalled Grass, "but Mitch decided to get the coverage from Federal Kemper (Life Assurance Company) with whom he was already doing business."

So it was simply prudent business advice that had convinced Portland real estate developer William M. "Mitch" Champagne to purchase a $1.5 million policy on his brother, Phillip, whom he had hired to oversee his rapidly expanding construction empire.

When Phil Champagne disappeared without a trace into the dark, cold waters off the San Juan Islands, Federal Kemper was understandably reluctant to release the money without a recovered body. Mitch demanded payment from Kemper on November 12, 1982 and filed suit to collect in May 1983. A settlement was reached, and in November 1983, Federal Kemper paid Champagne's company $700,000.

According to court documents, "Federal Kemper paid less than the face amount of the policy in the context of substantial uncertainty in the fact of Phillip Champagne's death."

When Phil turned up alive and imprisoned in 1992, the insurance company sued Mitch to recover, claiming a settlement condition required Mitch Champagne to repay the money if his brother was ever found alive. Mitch Champagne resisted the suit because a seven-year "enforceability period" had expired before it was filed.

"Mitch Champagne first learned his brother was alive when Federal Kemper served him with a summons for the insurance company's lawsuit," explained his lawyer, Henry Kantor, of Portland. "Mitch's reaction upon learning his brother was alive was absolute astonishment, which soon gave way to anger."

While Federal Kemper would appreciate having the money returned, Kemper's legal representative, Peter Richter, acknowledged that the insurance company made no claim of fraud in its lawsuit against Mitch Champagne.

While Mitch had been devastated by his brother's death, Phil's high-profile resurrection added legal insults to emotional injury.

"Mitch finds this entire situation humiliating and embarrassing," elaborated Mitch's attorney, Henry Kantor. "He lost his brother twice: once when Phil fell overboard and again when he resurfaced as a criminal. After ten years of grieving over the loss of his younger brother, he discovered that he had been deceived. Mitch is a victim of Phil's deception and, as far as I know, the brothers haven't spoken since Phillip turned up alive."

When the unexpected resurrection of Phil Champagne hit the headlines, the mavens of media collided in the halls of justice. Tabloids, talk shows, and first-run syndication television productions pushed the strange case of Phil Champagne to the top of their most-wanted list. Everyone wanted a salable piece of the not-so-dead deceased.

Including his two bereaved daughters.

Kathy and Renee, a Champagne pair of opportunistic offspring, steadfastly refused to grant even the most minimal press interviews. The reason cited for their icy silence was far from their Uncle Mitch's understandable aversion to public humiliation—they wanted money.

Barbara LeHew Fraley, a longtime companion of Harold Richard Stegeman of Hayden Lake, Idaho, had never heard of Phil Champagne, his brother Mitch, his daughters Kathy and Renee, or Federal Kemper Life Assurance Company. From October 1987 until debts and overhead put them out of business in 1990, she, Harold and her five children from a previous marriage had run Barb's Country Kitchen Restaurant along State Route 3 between Shelton and Bremerton, Washington.

On November 6, 1991, Harold, Barb, and her son, Richard, stopped for breakfast in Ritzville, Washington, at Perkins Restaurant. Located sixty miles southwest of Spokane along Interstate 90, Perkins has built its reputation on pancakes. After a pleasant meal, Barb paid for their ticket with a hundred dollar bill Harold had given her.

It was counterfeit.

Dragged from the pancake house in handcuffs, Barb pleaded ignorance. Harold went home to destroy evidence.

He failed.

Four months later, on Thursday, March 12, 1992, a state department investigator obtained a warrant to search the home of Harold Stegeman. While searching Stegeman's briefcase for evidence of Stegeman's identity, agents found a negative of a seal used on U.S. currency plus other evidence linked to counterfeiting. What the State Department had initially been looking for was Stegeman's passport.

They had already determined that a Harold Richard Stegeman had been born at University Hospital in Coral

Gables, Florida, on June 20, 1937, to Paul and Marie Stegeman. Paul Raymond Stegeman and the former Marie Elizabeth Leugers, both from Hamilton, Ohio, had migrated to Miami eight years earlier and resided at 3622 SW 25th Street. Paul was the proud proprietor of Stegeman Jewelry Store, specializing in watch repair.

Harold Stegeman was a student in the third grade at St. Theresa Elementary School when lung problems compelled him to spend seven days in Miami's Jackson Hospital. The State Department investigation revealed that Harold Stegeman died on November 3, 1945, at the age of eight years, four months, and fourteen days.

State Department investigators suspected that the adult male calling himself Harold Stegeman had also used the alias Frank Wincheski when he purchased photo-engraving supplies from Inland Photo Supply Company in Spokane. These supplies were later utilized in a counterfeiting operation run by the man who claimed to be Harold Stegeman.

Be he Frank or Harold, Barb's tall, dashing, and debonair beloved was a creative piece of work: a fraudulently obtained United States passport, fabricated identification and driver's license, hundred dollar bills which he had painted in an Idaho shed, and fingerprints matching those of a respectable, albeit deceased, Portland businessman named Phil Champagne.

Barb Stegeman and her five children had two good reasons to be dismayed. First, she was on trial for passing bogus bills. Second, she had been unceremoniously informed that her husband was counterfeit as well.

"Nothing would surprise me now," wept a sorrowful Mrs. Stegeman to an alternately stunned and bemused jury. "My husband could be involved in murder or anything as far as I know."

Richard Sanger, Barb's court-appointed attorney, outlined her defense in simple terms–she didn't know the bills that Harold had given her were counterfeit. Harold was going to testify on her behalf, but the revelation that Harold wasn't Harold didn't make him an ideal witness.

The jury found Barb Stegeman guilty. Released while she awaited sentencing, Barb and Harold were reunited.

"I married a man, not a name," insisted the loyal spouse of Harold Stegeman. Harold, Frank, Pete, and/or Phil wept with joy.

The Secret Service could tell stories about Harold Stegeman to rival the best pulp adventure fiction, but they won't. That's why they're called the Secret Service.

Created in 1865 as part of the Treasury Department, the Secret Service was established to defend the integrity of United States currency. As any amateur anarchist knows, one of the quickest ways to unravel an economy and the government that backs it is to create one's own unauthorized government-issue notes.

Harold Stegeman, however, was not and is not an anarchist, amateur or otherwise, and he will gladly tell stories about the Secret Service, the art of counterfeiting, how to acquire a U.S. passport with fraudulent identification or helpful survival tips for your next shoot-out with international smugglers. He also knows everything about the strange death of Phil Champagne.

Phil Champagne's children, Kathy, Renee, Phillip Jr., and Curtis, wept during the memorial service held in his honor at Portland's Little Chapel in the Chimes. Phil's younger brother, John Robin, was not invited. He had been the last man to speak to Phil alive and his parting words to Phil were these: "I never want to see you again."

"The day didn't start on such an unpleasant note," notes the once deceased Mr. Champagne. "John Robin, Larry Wills, an old high school pal of Mitch's from Boise, Idaho, and I got together for a few days of boating and fishing in the beautiful San Juan Islands. Mitch also invited our buddy, Ed Grass, but at the last minute, both Mitch and Ed had to cancel out."

"John, Mitch, and Phil Champagne were like real brothers to me," recalled Grass. "They are wonderful, kind, hardworking men who always treated me with the most kindness and friendship. I had been with them before on that beautiful forty-two foot Westsail—the *Warlock*—and I was supposed to be with them that weekend. A family matter came up and I couldn't go, but," said Grass with a sigh, "I often wonder if things would have gone differently if Mitch and I had been with the boys that night."

The boys–Phil, Larry, and John–did not travel together to the San Juans.

"Phil called Thursday to say he was meeting Larry Wills and would like to take him fishing and sailing," recounts John Robin. "I explained I had a prior commitment to take Jim Hinson and his family sailing, but that they would return to Portland on Sunday afternoon."

Saturday, Phil drove up Interstate from Portland through Olympia and Tacoma to meet Larry's Saturday flight from Boise at Sea-Tac International. Arriving in Anacortes, Washington, the two men rented a room for the night at the Gateway Motel.

The following day, while they waited for John Robin to arrive, Phil and Larry asked the Gateway's owner, Gerald Simon, for permission to re-enter the room to watch a ball game. They promised not to make a mess or cause any trouble. Mr. Simon agreed.

Uniting at the *Warlock* about an hour after the Hinsons had left, the three men had drinks at The Harbor, a little restaurant on the right side of Main Street going into town.

"Then we picked up a pizza from another place on the same side of the street," continues John Robin.

"They didn't serve any beer or wine, so we went back to the boat to eat the pizza and go to bed."

The next day, after an early breakfast, Larry Wills bought seasick pills in preparation for their afternoon fishing excursions to Cypress Island. Larry didn't get sick, and they caught one sand shark and one small cod.

By nightfall, the hot August day, augmented by chips and beer, had cooled to balmy island warmth. Phil, Larry, and John Robin returned to Anacortes and tied up in front of Boomer's Landing next to Wyman's Marina overlooking Guemes Channel.

"Phil fell when jumping from the boat to the dock because of his street shoes. I repeatedly tried to get him to wear a pair of my deck shoes," insists John Robin, "but they were a little small for him, so he wouldn't wear them."

Seated in the terraced dining room of Boomer's Landing, the men dined on steaks, chicken, pasta, and salad. Phil and Larry consumed impressive amounts of alcohol while John Robin stayed sober and flirted with cocktail server Linda Carlson. He did his best to convince her of the potential benefits of joining them aboard the *Warlock*. Having heard similar pitches and being a married woman, she simply waved good-bye as the three men motored out into the darkness.

Once they returned to the boat, John Robin switched fuel tanks and bled the engine. The winds were light, but he raised the sail to help steady the boat and increase fuel economy. Aboard the *Warlock*, Phil and Larry, over John's objections, began drinking vodka.

"I was a bit drunk, and I know Larry was also. It was a very relaxing day, and I had a marvelous time," relates Champagne, squinting into the horizon as if seeing 1982's San Juan Islands' sunlight dancing and sparkling on the waves. "I enjoyed John, Larry, the weather, the food, the drink. It was the first time I'd had any fun in a long while.

"My wife Joanne and I, after twenty-eight years, had hit significant skids in our relationship. Hell, we had been sliding toward separation for some time. We would have done it sooner, but a promise is a promise, and I take promises seriously. We waited 'til the kids were grown."

Attorney Don Robertson, a silver-haired Mount Rushmore of a man who at one time or another has represented almost every member of the Champagne family, describes Joanne Champagne as "a good mother and hardworking woman. She has always been more conservative and down-to-earth than Phil. Perhaps you would call her old-fashioned, more straight-laced. Some might consider her not as refined as Phil or say that they were a mismatched couple or that she is not the type of woman you would imagine to be Phil Champagne's wife. It is true that they had problems, but I have a great deal of respect and affection for Joanne Champagne."

Others are less generous in their appraisal of Phil's ex-better half.

"She was always unpredictable in her responses to situations," observes John Robin, "you never knew what to expect. She could be perfectly sweet and happy one minute and screaming the next. Maybe there was a medical explanation, but it seemed to me that her mood swings were dramatic and intense."

Then again, maybe Phil made her crazy.

"I had seen her verbally abuse him and insult him in public," recalled John Robin, "but because I was so happily married at the time, I couldn't relate to Phil's unhappiness in the relationship. As my brother has never been perfect, I'm sure she had complaints about him, too."

The children were not unaware of their mother's darker side.

"My kids all love their mother very much and would

do anything to protect her, but they all know that she can be verbally abusive and say things that cut like a knife. Even they had to be careful not to talk too much because she would get paranoid and accuse them of conspiring against her."

A few years before the boating accident, Phil confided to his daughter Renee that he wanted to leave Joanne and begin a new life. The idea was not greeted with enthusiasm.

"She told me that all the kids would hate me forever," said Champagne, "and I am sure they were concerned about what would happen to Joanne if I left."

The Champagne household was never the scene of physical abuse or domestic violence. The backlog of emotional bruises from decades of acerbic tirades resulted only in emotional distance and barren stretches of icy silence.

In June 1980, Phil moved out of the family home at 19202 S.E. Bel-Air in Clackamas, Oregon, and rented a small apartment in Gresham about ten miles east of the city limits of Portland. After the split, Phil began killing time and assassinating his sensibilities in Portland's nightspots.

Downshifting from his usual higher class haunts of the Gresham Golf Course, the Cattle Company, Top of the Cosmos, and the Rusty Pelican to some of the metro area's tougher night spots, he exchanged exaggerated and semi-fictional adventure stories with the rough and tumble of diverse locales and questionable people.

Having seldom walked on the wild side since his restless youth, Phil circled these new acquaintances, as would an entomologist approaching new species of scorpion. Half-lit in the dank glow of piratical rum, acting out against the wine-stained backdrop of false front camaraderie, the shiftless, daring-eyes piranhas appeared benignly picaresque.

By the time the music stopped and the bars closed down, Phil had returned to his rented digs. Unlike the wagering braggarts who provided his evening entertainment, Phil had a real job, reliable income, young adults who called him Dad, and friends in high places. What Phil Champagne shared with these unkempt nocturnals was self-induced internal numbness and the sensation of being buried alive by the future.

Phil's attraction to the sizzled denizens of Portland's soggy underworld was not a desire to be part of them, but to be disconnected from himself. In truth, he saw them for what they were—arrested adolescents delaying the detention of adulthood. At fifty-two, Phil had begun serving the life sentence of assumed maturity long ago.

Working in construction, living in constriction, Phil Champagne appreciated any inference of escape. One night, with deadpanned seriousness, he dutifully wrote down the phone numbers given which offered Phil a possible connection to a man in Mexico.

"The more Jim Beam this guy consumed, the better friend I became," laughed Phil. "I let down my guard, and it slipped that I would just as soon start a new life, not that I had any plans to do so, and he said, 'I know a man in Mexico who would probably be happy to have a man like you working for him.'"

The contact was someone who could use a fellow of Phil's talents and maturity in what sounded to be, at best, a dubious import/export enterprise. Phil did not intend to pursue the recommendation, but it tickled him to know he possessed private phone numbers radiating an aura of successful illegality.

"We didn't know each other that well, but as we had been introduced socially through this character's attorney, a lawyer with whom we both conducted perfectly legal and respectable business, he must have thought I was a real good ol' boy."

The man making the referral fell into the social strata best described as "smudged-collar worker"—white-collar appearance, but with dirt underneath more than his nails. He pretended not to be surprised when Phil asked, "What's the number?"

Champagne took down the area code and particulars on the back of a napkin, stuffed it into his inside pocket for later disposal, and changed the topic.

Three days later, when Phil Champagne pulled the crumpled napkin out of his pocket, he hesitated before tossing it in the trash. "What the hell," Phil thought, and copied the numbers into his address book.

"I can't say why I did it. Maybe it gave me a cheap ego thrill to know I had this guy's number."

The episode held sufficient significance for Champagne to share it with his buddy, Alias Mike.

Alias Mike is an alias for damn good reasons. The story of Phil Champagne began with his early and unexpected death, but over the years of his absence, the body count rose.

"Mike said I should have flushed the napkin down the sewer before I left the bar."

Mike was right.

As usual, he understood Phil's mental condition. The two men had shared an unspoken psychic symmetry since their prepubescent bonding as seventh-grade classmates in Lake Forest Park, a once rural community north of Seattle.

In April 1946, when fifteen-year-old Phil lied about his age to join the Merchant Marines, Alias Mike was right there with him. So was their school chum, John LeGate, and John LeGate had a younger sister named Joanne. Joanne had no intention of joining the Merchant Marines, but Phil had every intention of joining Joanne.

"My, oh my," said Champagne with a smile, "I thought little Joanne LeGate was a knockout."

Joanne waved good-bye when Phil, Mike, and her brother John shipped out for Europe aboard the *Marine Dragon* in 1946. A year later Phil found himself aboard *Foss Tug LT377* heading for Honolulu to bring back postwar explosives, and on November 8, 1949, Phil Champagne married Joanne LeGate in a simple ceremony at a preacher's house in Ridgecrest, Washington.

"Joanne was a beautiful bride and," he adds with a hint of impishness, "she was only a little bit pregnant."

Having returned to their old stomping grounds, Phil and his new brother-in-law's stomping quickly got out of hand. On November 27, 1950, the hell-raising, twenty-year-old boys went on a late-night spree, upending tombstones and breaking windows. The King County authorities were not amused. Le Gate and Champagne were apprehended, fingerprinted, and charged with property damage. They were ordered to make restitution and donate one hundred dollars to Orthopedic Hospital.

It was agreed that it would be best if the boys shipped out. Phil finished out 1950 working in Washington's Christmas tree harvest, and in 1951, he and John LeGate sailed aboard the *General Greeley* through the Panama Canal to New York City. As advised, they took a long, leisurely train ride from the East Coast back to the state of Washington.

And like *The Cat in the Hat*, the boys came back. Phil Champagne returned as restless, rowdy, and charming as when he was fifteen, with an emphasis on restless and rowdy, the natural consequences of Phil Champagne's haphazard upbringing.

Born in Seattle, the product of the stormy union of Eli and Anita Champagne, Phil's parents were separated at the time of his birth. Fourteen years later, Eli and Anita were officially divorced. Phil and his brothers were raised in poverty, relied on welfare grants for support, and constantly shifted from one home to another.

Anita Champagne and her middle son did not exemplify the finer points of family unity, and fifteen-year-old Phil was referred to the Seattle Guidance Clinic in 1945 because of problems with his mother. With her blessing, he joined the Merchant Marines in an attempt to jump start adulthood. By the early 1950s, Phil was supposed to be a grownup.

"I was a married man with a family to support, but I behaved like an irresponsible teenager," admitted Champagne. "I hadn't matured a whit. And to prove it, on June 9, 1945, I got drunk and took someone's new car for an extended joyride. When I was done with it, I parked it and walked away. The next morning, when I sobered up, I couldn't find my wallet. I went back to the car to see if I had left it there. It turned out I had left my wallet at the gas station when I bought a buck's worth of gas. The gas station attendant turned it over to the cops, who staked out the car. So, there I was, under arrest."

And guilty as hell.

This time, however, he wasn't a wild teen knocking over tombstones. He was an adult who had been caught taking a motor vehicle without authorization. The wife was furious, the judge was not sympathetic, and Phil was sentenced to one year at the correctional institute in Monroe, Washington.

As far as Joanne was concerned, the time, not to mention the behavior, could not have been worse. Their first child Kathy was only a toddler, and Joanne was pregnant with their second.

"Being sent to Monroe was a life-changing experience," admitted Champagne. "I grew up in a hurry. Renee was born while I was behind bars and that really had an impact on me. It was like slapping me upside the head. You never saw a guy change so fast in your life."

Released from Monroe a model of contrition, a more mature Phil Champagne migrated to Oregon with his family and joined Mitch as an employee of Carnation Dairy.

"Phil was one amazing milkman," laughs John Robin, implying that Phil's delivery route was an unending symphony of rattling bottles and squeaking bedsprings.

Becoming a licensed pasteurizer, Phil devoted ten good years to Arden Farms before following John Robin into construction.

Phil built homes while he and Joanne expanded their family. After four children and nearly three decades of marriage, the family painfully collapsed as the housing market did the same.

In 1982, Phil Champagne was no longer a teenager. He was over fifty, his unrelenting optimism and self-confidence were beginning to ebb, and his friends were concerned.

"It was easy to see that Phil was becoming increasingly stressed out and needed a few fun-filled days of fishing, sunshine, and friendship," Ed Grass said, "and we all hoped that the late August trip to the San Juans would do the trick."

The trick was not what anyone expected.

"When we started slicing through the night water, I felt like a free man," said Champagne wistfully. "There we were, a little tipsy, out on the water. I don't remember our destination, but we were near the Straits of Juan de Fuca. I had sneaked another bottle of vodka on board and was still drinking. John Robin didn't like folks getting drunk on the boat, but I didn't get much of a chance to cut loose and have a good time. So what if Larry and I got a little drunk?"

Even the most pleasant evening, fermented in enough alcohol, will turn sour. Old-timers have a name for it: The Darker Drink—the one shot that puts the pall of death on a lively night, turns fellowship into fistfights, loosens petty demons stuck in men's craws, and sets brother against brother.

"Somehow we got on the subject of Mitch's latest construction project—the Cottonwood Condominium development in a Portland suburb. There had been severe cost overruns because of some drainage problems, which we had not anticipated. I was the one to oversee the site, so, according to John, it was my oversight." Phil pauses for a moment of reflection. "It was a stupid discussion for two brothers, one of them rather tipsy, to be having in front of a friend on a boat in the dark of night. Had Mitch been there, he would have told us both to shut up."

Phil peered blearily at John Robin through the dark, weaving in rhythm with the rocking boat.

"You're trying to make Mitch's problems all my fault," declared Phil with the conviction of a man inebriated. "Don't blame me for things I can't control."

Blame is important to drunks and lawyers.

"The last thing I remember John saying," recalled Phil, "is that he didn't want to see me again. He turned and started to go either below or to the wheel. He stopped and turned back to look at me."

"D'ya know what?" John, despite his sobriety, let the Darker Drink speak. "If the truth were known, I don't think any of the others in the family want to see you again either."

John certainly knew how to put a positive cap on a night of carefree camaraderie.

"I did tend to criticize Phil," acknowledged John Rubin, "but I don't recall my recriminations being that severe. I usually knew just how far I could push Phil before he got mad or hurt, because Phil was very easygoing and slow to anger. Quite often, my fault-finding would do him some good. We did have that conversation, and I did say those things, but I think that the alcohol amplified the intensity with which he experienced it. If he'd taken my repeated insistence that he put on deck shoes as seriously as he took my remarks about his role in the construction site problems, he might not have gone over the side."

Phil, sizzled, silent, and still in his street shoes, turned toward the stern. He really didn't know where he was going.

He went overboard.

When John Robin caught the brief blur of Phil falling, he wasn't immediately concerned.

"My initial reaction was, 'Well, that's going to wake his ass up, hitting that cold water.' I stopped the boat, turned it around, and thought I would be able to see him right away."

He didn't.

John Robin grabbed a handheld searchlight and jumped down from the wheel, still confident that he would see Phil at any moment.

"I couldn't see him anywhere. I had a life ring on the back of the boat and a strobe light. I took the damn life ring, attached the strobe light, turned it on, and dropped it in to mark the spot. I was worried about the current and how we were drifting. Then I went below and called the Coast Guard, told them that I had a man overboard, had marked the spot, and that we were circling. It took them between twenty minutes and an hour to show up."

Larry Wills, previously pleasantly inebriated, was transformed into a panic-stricken drunk on deck.

"He was out of it, frantic, and flailing around. I was afraid Larry was going to fall overboard also. But he got a grip on himself in a hurry, and even though he had been drinking heavily, was able to steer. He suggested we shut the engine off and sail whenever possible so we would hear better if Phil was yelling."

The Coast Guard helicopter was aided in its search by the cutter *Polar Sea*. The search lasted thirteen hours.

Recalling the details of the agonizing night, John

Champagne fights back a flood of conflicting emotions.

"I know now that it wasn't real, that he didn't die. But it was real to me then, and real to me every day and every night since it happened. I have relived all of it over and over again, year after year. The fear, the prayers, the grief. I've gone over every detail of that night in my mind a thousand times," laments John Champagne. "What could I have done differently, how could I have saved my brother's life?"

There were several fishing boats in the immediate vicinity, but only one of them displayed interest in the search by assisting the *Polar Sea*.

"After the first hour," John's voice stalls as the memory constricts his larynx, "I knew that we were only looking for a body."

Even sober, an athletic swimmer can be deceived to death in dark waters, explained the Coast Guard. Rather than relaxing and floating to the surface, the natural inclination is to swim against the resistance toward safety. Phil Champagne, it was speculated, swam down rather than up. In truth, Phil Champagne didn't swim anywhere at all.

"I remember hitting the water, but if I had a near-death experience I was too drunk to remember it. I do recall wondering if this is what it was like for Dad."

Champagne's father, Eli Mitchell Champagne, drowned in Washington's Blue Lake when Phil was in his teens.

"If my life was going to pass before my eyes, I wasn't that interested," quipped Phil. "I have never been a fan of reruns, and it wasn't that great the first time around."

Sometimes men make light of what is most important. Phil didn't see the light; he only saw meaningless humdrum repetition in his ordered, rapidly vanishing life as he sank into wet, relentless darkness.

"What had I ever done that was worth a damn?"

What had I accomplished in my life? Nothing, I thought, nothing at all. Get married, have kids, raise kids, get old, get sick, die. Big deal."

No one was about to offer Phil Champagne a counseling job at a hospice, but it was his life, his death, his self-evaluation.

"If I had died, it was no big loss. I felt that what came next must at least be different."

Phil Champagne stared death in the face and found the face of a ten-year-old boy staring back.

"Hey, Mom. The man woke up," the boy said.

Champagne's consciousness resurfaced in a child's bedroom. Phil saw toys and other obvious indications of preadolescence, an odd collection of stuffed animals and posters of popular sports figures. Phil had seen these same things in his own boys' rooms.

When his youngest son, Curtis, turned twenty, he had stopped looking at Daddy with the same eyes. If there was blame to be attached, Phil was no longer drunk enough to attach it.

The child's attractive, forty-something mother appeared briefly in the doorway. She smiled, turned, and walked away. Phil heard her use the phone. He knew it was a phone. He recognized the rotary dial.

"Rotary dial. Rotary dial. The name sounds exactly like what it is," Phil spoke to himself, but his lips didn't move. "If you say 'rotary dial,' there is exactly one click for every letter; it takes the exact amount of time to say 'rotary dial' as it does to dial the zero."

He attempted to sit up.

He failed.

He tried to call out but was not sure if sound escaped his throat. For a moment, he wondered if he was invisible, but then recalled both the child and the woman had seen him. It had seemed a reasonable question when it first occurred to him. Maybe he had the flu. Maybe he was delirious. Maybe he was dead. It was too complicated.

The boy continued to stare at the rumpled man, while the man stared at the ceiling. The kid-sized bed barely contained the long, lanky frame of Phil Champagne. The little boy had never before seen a man sleep with his eyes open. The man must be asleep, the child reasoned, because dead men don't cough, moan, and call out names.

"I see you're back among the living." A cheerful male voice commanded Phil's attention and dominated the room. Champagne blinked, bringing his open eyes into focus. He didn't know the voice, didn't know the face. He didn't have the slightest idea where on earth he was.

"At first we thought you were dead."

Champagne's mind attempted to unravel the intricacies of the situation, but the situation wasn't all that intricate. A bearded, roughhewn man in jeans, Pendleton shirt, and black boots filled the doorway with his broad shoulders. Flipping open a Zippo, the man brought the bluish flame to the Lucky Strike trapped between his lips. Phil, after the first decade or the first puff, whichever came sooner, understood that the smoking bearded man was attempting to make conversation.

"You must be Art," mumbled Phil stupidly.

"Art?" The man in the door with smoke pouring out his nose didn't understand.

"Art of Lost Conversation." Phil hated explaining a joke.

"You're been here almost four days," offered the beard. "When I first found you, I thought you were dead. You know I fished you out of the water, right?"

Oh, yeah, the water. It was starting to come off pause and slip into rewind. Playback and paybacks were imminent.

Reclining beneath a poster of Luke Skywalker, Phil

propped himself up on his elbows as if a clear line of sight would encourage his brain to realign as well.

"Why didn't you—?" Phil wasn't sure what he was about to ask.

"Take you to a hospital? Well, there's a reason for that. In fact, a couple of good reasons," the bearded, smoking dragon of the doorway, spit a piece of errant tobacco from the tip of his tongue. "I had fish and plenty of 'em, but I am not exactly authorized to be catchin' 'em, if you understand. I was willing to save your life, but not willing to maybe lose my boat."

"I could have died," Phil said, intending a manly bark but gave out only a weak, watery yelp. "Exactly where am I?"

"Anacortes, Washington, or at least reasonably close to it. We're not that far from town. Here, you might want to take a look at this." Pulling a newspaper from under his arm, the bearded fisherman stepped forward. Champagne looked to where the man pointed. "Seems like folks figure you're dead."

It was hard for Phil to focus his attention, let alone his vision, but he understood without having to read the details.

"You didn't have no wallet. But you're the only missing man I know of that ain't missing in this house, so that's you, right?"

"I need to use the phone. I gotta tell somebody I'm alive," Phil said. His voice bore equal traces of desperation and disorientation.

"No phone here," the beard lied. "Tomorrow you can call from town. Your clothes are dry and so's your money."

Phil had forgotten about the money. He always kept cash in his pocket, figuring it was easier to lose your wallet than your pants.

"We don't steal in this family. Helping ourselves to

fish provided by nature is one thing. Lifting a helpless man's cash is another. And we ain't askin' you to give us any of it neither. Just keep it between us that you were ever here."

"Yeah…" Phil wondered if it was a delirium-induced illusion or if he was really having a conversation.

"You look like you're driftin', pal. You sleep some more, and in the morning I'll take you into Anacortes and you can give your people a call or whatever suits you."

Phil leaned back and closed his eyes. "I'll need a shave…"

Whatever additional considerations he was about to voice disappeared in the darkness of exhaustion.

TWO

Life being what it is in our world, the onset of death is often the first taste a man gets of freedom.

—Isaac Rosenfeld

Eighty hours after the United States Coast Guard called off its thirteen-hour search for John Champagne's missing brother, the aromas of sizzling bacon, fried eggs, and fresh brewed coffee awakened the assumed deceased.

Phil Champagne—showered, shaved, and dressed—cleaned his plate and heard the insistent jingle of the bearded man's keys well before he had swallowed his final triangle of toast. If this was the bum's rush, at least the bum was well fed.

The fisherman's old blue pickup rattled along the blacktop road into the Fidalgo Island city of Anacortes. The beard noted that it was easy to forget that Anacortes was on an island as the ridges connecting it to the mainland made the transition appear seamless. Except for the brief exchange about the geography of the area, the balance of the ride consisted of interpersonal silence punctuated by an occasional gear grind or the metallic flip of the Zippo.

"This is it," said the beard with stoic finality as he pulled over to a downtown curb. "You never saw me; I never saw you."

"Yeah."

Phil yanked at the passenger side's reluctant handle, opened the dented door, and stepped out. He stood for a moment, shifting his weight awkwardly, not quite knowing what to say to the man who had saved his life. As words didn't come, he didn't say anything. The blue pickup simply moved on down the road.

"Okay, so I didn't thank the guy. Looking back, I can see that I wasn't thinking with perfect clarity. I was irked at him for not taking me to the hospital. I could have died there in his cabin, but as he said, 'You're alive, ain't ya, so what are ya complainin' about?'"

Phil watched the pickup become a distant blue blur and turned his attention back to himself. He needed a change of clothes, transportation, and a clear head. Despite more than three days of bed rest, his weariness amazed him. Limp pasta legs and an unrelenting lightheadedness compelled Phil to wobble when he walked. He stopped every half block to steady himself.

"It's not like I had any idea where I was going. There I was, weaving around like a man either going into or coming out of shock, no ID, and a pocketful of cash. On top of all that, I'm missing and presumed dead."

In the mind of his daughter, Renee, Phil was missing and presumed murdered. Following the news of her father's death, she placed an emotional call to the United States Coast Guard alleging that her Uncle John plotted to kill Phil for the insurance money. As John was not a beneficiary of any policy, but Renee was, her accusation was summarily discounted. Later, coming to her senses, Renee apologized to her Uncle John.

Her mother, however, retained Don Robertson to sue John Robin for negligence in the wrongful death of Phil Champagne. Joanne was awarded $8,500 in an out-of-court settlement.

"On top of the pain of losing my brother," recounts

John Robin, "I had to deal with accusations of murder and lawsuits of negligence. One day I'm taking my brother and a friend for a boat ride, and the next I'm treated like a criminal."

It is no crime to be alive. The Anacortes police had received no APB to be on the lookout for a law-abiding, waterlogged refugee from the briny deep, answering the description of Phillip Wendell Champagne, weaving down Commercial Avenue with $1,400 in his pocket.

Phil aimed his unsteady gait toward the first visible coffee shop, sat down in an available booth, and attempted deep thoughts. His success was spotty at best.

"I think that's when it hit me," said Phil. "I remembered that last painful conversation with John; 'It's all your fault, everything is your fault, all of Mitch's problems are your fault, we never want to see you again,' and all that crap. Well, it pissed me off and I was like a kid who decides to take his ball and go home or grabs his Teddy bear and a peanut butter sandwich and starts walking, except I wasn't a kid. Yeah, that was it, all right—if they didn't want to see me again, they sure as hell didn't have to."

Before a man can steal, he has to lie; before a man can lie, he has to justify it to himself. Phil Champagne spent the better part of his time in Anacortes engrossed in justifications.

"I figured no one would starve to death if I wasn't around. I was leaving my wife and kids, but she didn't like me anyway. As far as I was concerned, she made my life a living hell. She probably felt the same about me. She accused me of every sin in the book. I have to admit that I wasn't the best husband in the world, but I did provide. Damn right. I always provided. As for the kids, they were grown-up and I managed to convince myself that they wouldn't care if I came home or not."

Champagne's voice catches briefly.

"I love them all," admitted Phil. "I knew I would miss them, but I pushed the discomforting thought that I would regret what I was doing to the back of my mind. I didn't want to go back to things the way they were. It was like I had been pulled out of the game and set on the sidelines. It was either go back on the field or leave the stadium."

Phil paid for the coffee, aimed for the exit, and ambled off in search of a clothing store.

"I bought three pairs of Haggar slacks, shirts, socks, underwear, belt, and a good pair of shoes. Then I picked out a small travel bag, packed it neatly, and added basic toiletries. By the time I started thumbing my way from Anacortes to Interstate 5, I was the cleanest, freshest, most affable looking hitchhiker you ever saw in your life."

Champagne got a quick lift to the I-5 southbound on-ramp. With his non-threatening adult demeanor, crisp clothes, and fresh look, a nonstop ride down the freeway to Seattle was no challenge.

A gregarious salesman in a four-door Oldsmobile attempted entertaining his appreciative passenger with wholesale anecdotes and off-color jokes while Phil deflected any direct questions as to his point of origin or final destination with vague generalities or hastily invented specifics. As a good host senses the discomfort of silence, the driver attempted to fill the void with a contemporary FM soundtrack.

Static.

"That's because of the shading effect of hills and trees," explained the driver. "The FM radio signals hit 'em and drop like a rock. Now, the old AM stations' signals will bounce around forever. They never go away. Send 'em out today, and even if it is a little, tiny 250-watt station, it never goes away; it just keeps bouncing. Why, I bet if you sat down late at night with a real strong

AM radio, you could hear old shows from the 1930s still floating back to earth."

"I must be one of those old AM signals," joked Phil Champagne, and the salesman laughed.

The conversation waned, the radio reception improved, and the two men rolled down the interstate past Marysville, Everett, and Mukilteo in air-conditioned comfort. On the outskirts of Lynwood, 96.5 FM cranked out "Heard it on the X."

Even Phil Champagne knew about the infamous "X," a radio station in Mexico with more power in its tower than any station in the U.S.A. Wolfman Jack used to be on the "X" selling autographed pictures of Jesus Christ.

Mexico sounded like Phil's kind of place.

The Oldsmobile hit heavier traffic passing Seattle's Northgate exit, slowed considerably by N.E. 85th, picked up briefly approaching the university district, slowed again at the 520 Interchange, and eased up as they took the Steward-Denny exit to downtown.

"You can just let me off anywhere here," said Phil. His stomach felt tight. Seattle was civilization in the way that Portland was civilization. Being unconscious, or in Anacortes, was like a respite in the Twilight Zone. Phil Champagne wasn't sure he was ready for reentry into reality.

"Hey, the bus depot is just down there. No problem, pal."

Handshakes, thanks, and a solid door slam later, Phil Champagne was standing in front of the Greyhound bus depot.

He walked in, looked around for the schedule, and discovered he had a good two hours until the next bus to Portland, Oregon.

"There was a little restaurant in the bus depot, or attached to it on the west side of the building on the corner, and I sat there drinking coffee and wondering if

I was doing the right thing, whatever the hell that was."

Phil purchased a one-way ticket to Portland, pumped a handful of change into a nearby pay phone, and dialed a number in Oregon, area code 503. He didn't call his estranged wife; he didn't call his kids, other, or brothers. He called Alias Mike.

"If his wife had answered, I would have hung up and tried later," confirmed Champagne, "but Mike picked up the phone. To say he was surprised to hear from me would be putting it mildly."

Mike was surprised to hear from his dead best friend, but not surprised by Phil's decision to stay dead.

"At first, Mike wasn't sure it was really me. I told him everything that happened, at least everything I could remember, and then I told him what I was going to do–stay dead and start over. I will never forget his response, 'It's about time you got out of that hellhole you're in anyway.'"

If Phil Champagne was seeking external validation of his decision to change his life, he got it on the pay phone. Whatever doubts lingered were dispelled the moment Mike uttered the word hellhole. That cinched it.

"We made plans to meet and set the location. I felt giddy when I climbed on the bus to Portland. The ride seemed to take forever, stopping at every would-be-depot down the I-5 corridor."

Tacoma, Fort Lewis, Olympia, Centralia, Longview, Vancouver; the opportunities to change his mind outnumbered the rest stops.

"I didn't believe I could change my mind. Once I was on that bus my only goal was to get two things from Portland—my address book and more money."

If there was anything unusual about the well-dressed passenger's behavior when he stepped off the Portland bus, it was the intensity with which he walked straight to the stately Benson Hotel.

"Mike was waiting for me in a dark corner at the back of Trader Vic's. He shook my hand, stared at me for a bit, and asked what I wanted first, advice or money. I told him I would take as much of both as he was willing to give."

It wasn't true. Phil wanted money and affirmation. He had seen a vision of his life with ice-like clarity. In a post-traumatic epiphany reserved for the mystic and the head-injured, he had broken the bonds and snapped the trap. Phil Champagne flew the coop of conventional expectations, embraced the implications of his own demise, and canceled his subscription to the resurrection.

Mike took a good look at his old pal Phil. The man had changed. There was an aura of renewed confidence. This was not the Phil Champagne he had recently seen sinking into a black hole of self-recrimination somewhere in Gresham. Champagne appeared a man possessed.

"It could have been worse," reasoned Mike. "At least he wasn't screaming about Jesus."

Mike correctly observed that Phil Champagne was not truly back from the dead; he was only dropping by for drinks.

"Sure, you can go away, change your name, start a new life somewhere. Maybe. But what about money, a job, a career? You are rapidly approaching old age." Mike laughed as if he were teasing. He wasn't. "You are over fifty."

Phil had his answer prepared, if not rehearsed, and didn't mind waiting for the Trader Vic's waiter to take their order before unloading his litany.

"Remember Smudge Collar, the import/export guy who said he knew where I could get a job?" Phil smiled as if he need say no more.

"Bullshit, Phil," insisted Mike. "That was pure, unadulterated bullshit—bullshit offer and bullshit for you to take down that number. You've got to be kidding."

"What do you mean, bullshit? He wouldn't have given me the number if he didn't mean for me to use it." Phil was convincing himself even as he spoke, pausing to allow the waiter to deliver his vodka and Mike's bourbon. "I want you to go to the condo I was building for Mitch and get my little book. It has a number I can call in Mexico City. I'll tell you exactly where my book is."

Mike banged his glass on the table, spilling a puddle beside the cocktail napkin. He looked around and wiped his mouth with his thumb and forefinger, stalling to stay calm.

"Honest to God, Phil. You better sleep on this. Besides," hissed Mike, "I'm not going out to those damn condos in the middle of the fucking night. I'll get it early in the morning, but I want you to get some sleep. Then we'll get you out of town."

"Yeah, get me out of town for sure. I don't want to hang around here. Shit, if someone sees me, I'll be a dead man."

They laughed at Phil's unintentional humor, breaking the tension born of emotional disagreement.

"I'll drive you to Salem in the morning, and you can catch the bus to wherever it is you wanna go from there."

"I just want to go..." For a fraction of a moment, Phillip Champagne didn't have the slightest idea.

He attempted to form the sentence again.

"I just want to go someplace where I can feel okay, never have to deal with Joanne again, and never do anything to piss off or disappoint my family, Mitch, John—anybody."

"I guess if gone, you can't do anything wrong," Mike commented dryly.

"Right about that," Phil agreed seriously. "I am never, ever again going to be in a position where someone can say Mitch's problems are all my fault. As for marriage..."

42

"Easy, Phil. I'm a happily married man. My wife and I get along fine."

Champagne snapped a swizzle stick between his fingers.

"That's right, Mike, rub it in. You are one in a million. I bet there are hundreds of thousands of men and women out there right now who feel just as I did before I died. Trapped, suffocated, tormented, blamed, shamed…," Phil ran out of words.

"Try reamed and creamed and a bit obscene," suggested Mike helpfully. Phil laughed and raised his glass in a silent toast.

"You're a good friend, Mike. I've got other good friends, too—Don Robertson, Ed Grass—but please don't tell them I'm alive. And for God's sake, don't tell my brothers."

"I'm not telling a single living soul as long as I live," vowed Mike. "Want another drink?"

"No," said Phil, soaking up Mike's spillage with the little Trader Vic's napkin, "I wouldn't want to go overboard."

"Yeah, overboard," chuckled Mike. "Speaking of which, don't go running away from one bad patch of aggravation into another with the Mexican deal. Watch your step. I don't want you to end up dead or making license plates. After all, your style has always been more Sheraton than Shelton."

Phil understood the alliterative reference easily enough. Shelton, population seventy-two hundred, located on an inlet of South Puget Sound near Olympia, Washington, is famed for Christmas trees, succulent oysters, and a penal institution called the Washington Corrections Center.

Phil had never attended the Shelton Oktoberfest oyster-shucking contest and considered "Correction Centers" an absurd euphemism. What would they

43

correct? Your spelling? Your golf swing? Phil was, however, intimately familiar with Shelton's Christmas tree harvest. Between late November and mid-December 1950, Phil cut, packaged, and shipped a portion of the three million Christmas trees exported from Shelton to happy homes throughout the region.

"I know the difference between Sheraton and Shelton," said Phil, "but do you know the difference between a sailor and a shower?"

"No."

"Well, you better find out before you get under one."

Mike laughed more from obligation than spontaneity. The conversation concluded and the drinks paid for, Phil and Mike arranged to meet in the morning then split up.

With neither a Sheraton nor Shelton in sight, Phil Champagne, using an assumed name, checked into the Hilton down the street, went up to the rather elegant room, and slid between the cool cotton sheets. In the morning, Mike would drive him to Salem, see him off with warm wishes and cold cash, and he would be free—free from providing, free from blame, free from responsibility for anyone or anything except himself.

On that September night in 1992, Phil Champagne slept the sleep of a man at peace. The Hilton was even better than the Sheraton, and both were better than Shelton.

Barbara LeHew Yokum Fraley of Olympia, Washington, was not so fortunate. Her sleep that night was fitful at best. As always, she said her prayers with heartfelt sincerity. That's how she was raised—believe in the Bible and the trust in God. Her upbringing was strict, religious, unflinching, and crowded—four brothers, two sisters, one mother, and no father.

Barb had become accustomed to hardship, but it was not her personal preference. She was never afraid of hard work, but she was becoming pretty darn tired of it.

She prayed for her kids; she prayed for herself. But, in the final analysis, it was up to her to provide for the five children from her failed thirteen-year-marriage to former Shelton inmate #222301, Richard Yokum, a.k.a. Richard Fraley.

When Barb married Richard Yokum in 1965, no one thought the naïve, estrogen-crazed eighteen-year-old girl had made the catch of the century. He was a soldier from Fort Lewis with a passion for the ladies and a proclivity for going AWOL. They met in 1974 at the Evergreen Ballroom, where Barb worked part-time in the cafeteria. The night Buck Owens performed, Barb had the evening off, and Richard discovered the girl of his dreams on the dance floor.

"Oh, he was a good-looking fellow, all right," said Barb with a laugh. "My mother forbade me to marry until I was eighteen. I was seventeen when I met Richard and fell madly in love. We were married a year later."

Richard was on probation.

"He had taken a succession of unsuccessful jobs after the Army invited him to leave," recounts Barb, "one of them being for a janitorial service which cleaned department stores, except Richard didn't just clean them. He cleaned them out—he took a television and some other items and pawned them. Not a smart move, and he got in big trouble."

That wasn't the end of it.

One year after Richard promised to love, honor, and cherish her forever, Barb was eight months pregnant with their first child and facing a prison sentence for forgery. Both the pregnancy and forgery were, according to Barb, the doing of Richard Yokum.

"He stole a woman's purse from a bowling alley, took the cash, and wanted me to sign her name for purchases using her credit card," relates Barb, minimizing her blatant criminal complicity. "When I was supposed to sign, I chickened out and ran out of the store. It was too late. They got me for forgery or attempted forgery or something. Then they came after me for stealing the purse. It wasn't me that stole the purse, it was Richard."

Richard recalled the purse-stealing incident as a collaborative effort.

"Had she not been with me," he admitted, "she would not have done it on her own."

"I was a foolish girl and up to no good," recalled the ex-Mrs. Yokum. "I can't say what sterling qualities I first saw in Richard besides his good looks and charming personality, but what I got from Richard right off the bat were pregnancy and imprisonment."

Barb insisted that her lawyer begged her to name Richard the father as Richard the purse-snatcher.

"But he'll go to jail," objected Barb.

"That," the lawyer explained, "is the whole idea."

Richard Yokum, who was already on probation, provided convincing descriptions of dire consequences for both her and the child should he be sent away.

Barb's lawyer talked her out of pleading guilty and instead launched a defense of innocent by reason of insanity. "He figured I had to be nuts," explained Barb ruefully.

The day her first baby was born, Barb went off for ten months to the county jail to await trial. The baby went off with Barb's mother. Barb got probation.

Richard Yokum's attempts to avoid incarceration proved equally fruitless. While Barb was in the county jail, he violated probation. Richard Yokum was sent to the correction center in Shelton. After release he violated parole and spent a year at the correction center in Monroe, Washington, where Phil had stayed in the early fifties, followed by a stay at the Washougal Honor Camp in 1971.

"Richard had been using the name Yokum because that was his grandparents' name, and they raised him," explained Barb. "But it turned out his legal name was Fraley, and that was the name on the baby's birth certificate, too. All of a sudden, I was Mrs. Fraley instead of Mrs. Yokum. When he applied for a job with the Washington State Department of Institutions in 1971, he did so as Richard Fraley."

The new and improved Richard worked the first three years as a counselor at the Rainier State School in Buckley, Washington, for what were then termed "retarded kids." He was then transferred to a similar position at Cascadia Diagnostic Center, a residential program for troubled juveniles. When Cascadia closed down, Richard Fraley relocated to Shelton's Washington Corrections Center, but this time not as an inmate.

If a leopard can't change its spots, Richard Yokum Fraley is the exceptional leopard. He became an exemplary employee of the Washington Corrections Center, if not a model husband, and built a rewarding career highlighted by consistent pay raises and promotions.

With Richard Fraley on the right side of the law, a good job, and promising future, things should have been peachy between Richard and Barb. He was, after all, an excellent provider. He was also a handsome devil who had a way with the ladies. The problem was in the plurality. According to Barb, Richard became increasingly indiscreet about where he parked his nightstick. After thirteen years of marriage, Barb and Richard agreed to divorce.

"As a mature, sober adult, Richard is not a bad guy at all," commented Barb. "I have no malice toward him. He never beat me, abused me, or anything like that, and when we were married, he always provided well for the kids and me. Maybe he was just too good looking for his own good. When Richard and I split up, it wasn't easy for anybody."

And Barb kept working. Her mother was in the restaurant business, and Barb knew her way around a kitchen. She worked two or three different jobs at once to support the kids.

Overworked, underpaid, and longing for true love, Barb Fraley, against her mother's deathbed wishes, remarried on April 30, 1983. The man was Cecil Chapman. Together, he and Barb moved to Shelton, where her new husband joined Richard on the right side of the bars at the Corrections Center, becoming her ex-husband's drinking buddy.

"I was the one in the wedding dress," quipped Barb, "but Cecil wound up with Richard."

After three years of what Barb terms "irreconcilable differences" fueled by Cecil's excessive alcohol consumption, there was nothing she wanted from Chapman except away. She didn't even retain his name. The kids were all Fraleys, so she stayed one, too.

A five-time mother and two-time divorcée, Barb never had the opportunity to take it easy. Since leaving Olympia's Washington Junior High at the age of fifteen to attend the live-in nurse's aide program at Saint Peter's Hospital, her life had been nonstop work punctuated by pregnancy, imprisonment, infidelity, and abuse. As a professional victim, Barb was ready for a career change.

In March 1986, while tending bar at Shelton's roadside Cottage Café, she met Harold Richard Stegeman. A tall, handsome man, his refined bearing marked him immediately as someone whose origin and upbringing were far removed from that of the locals. Harold was a man with class.

On his first visit to the Cottage Café, Harold sat with a local real estate agent hacking out the details for the sale of a cabin he was building on nearby Harstine Island. On subsequent visits, Harold found more delight in the presence of Ms. Fraley than in any item on the menu. They had short, relaxed chats as she refilled his coffee. He spoke of the cabin he was building and his recent retirement from a successful career in Florida real estate. He had never been married, never had kids. Wistfully, Barb dreamed that she could change that part of his story.

Three weeks after their initial encounter, Harold waited around the Cottage café until Barb's shift was over to ask her out on a Friday night date. She hesitated a few seconds before responding—not from doubt as to her answer, but out of complete surprise.

"When Harold asked me out, I was in total shock. I never in a million years thought he would look at me twice. My self-esteem was gone. I no longer considered myself attractive, and I was nobody but the mother of five children."

Flattered, she joyously accepted.

Pensive about his acceptance of her five children, she made no mention of them during their first few evenings together. In time Barb decided to reveal their existence, but prefaced her self-conscious disclosure with the observation that Harold might not ever want to date her again once he knew "the truth."

"I have five kids," Barb told him holding up her hand with all five fingers spread wide, "and I do mean five."

Barb held her breath. Harold laughed. He already knew. When he had picked her up for their first date, he saw the noses pressed against the front window. Harold could count.

After six months of romantic dating, Harold, Barb, and the remaining three minor children began cohabitation. Harold treated her with respect, cared for her deeply, and was seriously concerned for her needs and the well being of her children. For the first time since her mid-teens, Barb didn't have to work. Her kids, accustomed to scraping by, hardly knew how to act around the kind, loving man who found simple, honest pleasure in making them happy.

Harold Stegeman built a house in the Mud Bay area near Olympia, sold it at a profit, and then, knowing Barb had an extensive background in restaurant and lounge management, financed Barb's Country Kitchen and Stegey's Blue Room just off the main highway between Shelton and Bremerton on Spencer Lake. Barb felt the remote location posed a significant risk, but Harold was convinced that the site was perfect for tourist traffic. Stegeman firmly believed that a well-run restaurant featuring delicious prime rib would be like having a license to print money.

With construction beginning on the restaurant, Harold bought a twenty-eight foot Mercruiser inboard/outboard Tollycraft boat so they would have something to do while their new venture was being built. They took the kids fishing all day and spent the night on the boat. The next morning they would find a nice place on the water to eat and enjoy a leisurely breakfast. Barb LeHew Fraley's prayers were no longer pleas for help, but prayers of praise and gratitude for the blessing in her life named Harold Stegeman.

The restaurant opened with hoopla and fanfare in October 1987. The food was delicious, the drinks generous, the service adequate, and Harold Stegeman became Shelton's resident high-profile tycoon. Everyone knew his story: "Mr. Moneybags fell in love with the local waitress and built her a restaurant all her own."

Soon after the grand opening, Harold also bought Barb a lovely five-bedroom house on the lake and a new car. On the weekends, Harold and Barb would travel to Seattle where he introduced her to the Sheraton Towers, Trader Vic's, and the famous Thirteen Coins.

"I had never been to places like that in my life,"

recalled Barb. "I felt like Cinderella at the ball. On New Year's Eve, Harold took me to a party at the Seattle Sheraton. He wore a tuxedo and had me fitted for an evening gown. An evening gown!" Barb repeats with a delightful combination of astonishment and glee.

Mom was right. Life was good. Believe in the Bible, trust in God, and good things come to those who wait. If it was a dream, Barb LeHew Fraley Stegeman never wanted to wake up. She would never go back. She was free at least—free to relax, free to enjoy, free to be the loving partner of Harold Richard Stegeman.

With the sun streaming through the windows of the downtown Portland Hilton, the world was bright with infinite possibilities for the newly awakened Phil Champagne. Room service delivered a delicious breakfast with plenty of fresh brewed coffee, and Phil had let the hot shower beat on his back for an eternity before getting out and drying off. He picked out a pair of the new Haggar slacks and a shirt from the wardrobe he had hung carefully in the closet of the Hilton buffed his new shoes, and whistled while he packed his travel bag. Walking to the window, Phil Champagne took in the view.

Portland looked more than ever like Portland—half a million people living in what was first called Stumptown. The name "Portland" was decided by an 1845 coin toss. If the coin had landed the other side up, Phil Champagne would be high-tailing it out of Boston, Oregon, instead of Portland.

Just for the hell of it, Phil flipped a coin. Heads it's Portland; tails it's Boston. Boston won.

"Shows what I know," said Phil. He pocketed the coin, picked up his bag, paid up, checked out, and met Mike right on time in the passenger load zone.

"Did you get my little book?"

"Yes, I got your little book with the name and number of the little crook. Now, let's get your sorry supposed-to-be-dead ass to Salem before someone bumps into you and has a goddamn heart attack."

Phil laughed, climbed in, and kicked back.

"Do you think I would be less conspicuous if I had a bag over my head?"

"Not less conspicuous, but better looking."

Portland's skyline glistened on Phil's right, I-5 stretched southbound before him, and his past was close behind.

"I'm not breaking any law, you know," remarked Phil as if there was some doubt. "It's no crime to be alive."

Mike nodded.

"It isn't like I'm deserting my wife and kids, either," Phil said as if someone in the car were giving him an argument. No one was giving Phil any argument.

"My wife and I are divorcing. The kids are adults. I'm not leaving anyone with any debts. Mitch will be better off without me, and…"

"And you just want to get the fuck out of Dodge," Mike said, whacking the steering wheel with the palms of his hands.

"Dodge? I want to get the fuck out of the entire state of Kansas!"

Both men laughed.

Gresham and Clackamas were long behind them when Phil asked Mike a question as if he really wanted an answer.

"Do you think I am doing the right thing?"

"The right thing for who?"

Phil wasn't sure.

"I mean, before I always played it safe. I never even would have just taken off if I hadn't…"

"Died?"

"Yeah. For some reason, that made a difference. I

could have walked away any day, driven off into any night, gone to the train yard and jumped a..."

"Waitress?"

"Dammit, Mike, you know..."

"Sure, I know lots of waitresses."

Phil slugged Mike in the shoulder.

"Hey, I'm drivin' here."

Silence.

Past the Canby off-ramp fifteen miles south of Portland, the conversation picked up again.

"Hey, Phil?"

"Yeah?"

"Did you ever read *The Maltese Falcon*?"

"*The Maltese Falcon*? Well, I saw the movie a few times on TV. It had Bogey and what's-his-name, Piper Laurie."

"Peter Lorre, you dumbshit. I saw the movie, too, but did you ever read the book?"

"Naw, why? Did it have hot parts they couldn't put in the film or something? I'm not crazy about smut unless I am experiencing it personally, you know."

"No, not smut, but the Sam Spade detective character tells this story about a guy kind of like you."

"Yeah?" Despite the air-conditioning, Phil cracked open the window.

"Ten years later they find the guy. He's not living faraway at all, and the thing is, this guy was miserable enough to just take off. And when they find the guy, his life is the same; he's doing the same kind of work and having the same kind of life he did before, so it's ten years later and he's exactly who he was. Only his name and location have changed."

"And what does that mean?"

"People are who they are, I guess. You know 'Wherever you go, there you are.'" Mike let the sentence hang like a spider web. "Where will you be in ten years?"

53

"Damned if I know, but I am looking forward to finding out." Phil squinted as if attempting to peer into the future. "Coasta Rica, India, Africa, Honduras…"

"McNeil Island, Walla Walla, Shelton…," continued Mike, naming well-known Pacific-Northwest penal institutions.

"Hey, I am not a crook," intoned Phil in his best imitation of Richard Nixon.

"Yeah, but deep down inside you're a wannabe crook. I always figured the only thing that stood between you and a failed life of crime was your essential stupidity plus a basic lack of creativity and a sincere shortage of guts," Mike teased.

"Gee, thanks," Phil said, growling.

"You start dealing with Mr. Mexico and his import business, and I'm afraid you'll be outclassed by lowlifes," Mike said with a laugh.

"Wait a second, Mike." Phil grew intense but not from anger. "What the hell else am I supposed to do? I have no identification, no Social Security number; I can't just go out and get a real job here. I have to leave the country to work. I figure it's like taking a nonunion gig. This guy made me an offer of low-risk, decent income, and it may be legal as hell when you get right down to it. It isn't like I am running off to join some goddamn organized crime family. I'm not some Hispanic Marlon fucking Brando, for God's sake. Give me a break. I'm not going to lead some South American revolution, and I don't even speak the language, *amigo*."

"That's a plus," observed Mike sardonically, "because Mexico is in North America. As for your language problem, every person you meet, just say '*Hijo de puta*,' and smile."

"Heave-ho and punt yourself, smartass. You got any real advice? What else can I do besides pasteurization, construction, and a damn good German accent?" said

Phil in a damn good German accent. "Tell me, Sergeant Pepper, can you see any other way?"

Mike knew it was of no use, even by a circuitous route, to attempt to change Phil's mind, so he changed the subject.

"Hey, if they ever make a movie of your life, who plays me?" asked Mike with a buoyant enthusiasm.

"Hmm," Phil gave the cinematic casting call serious consideration. "How about Joey Heatherton?"

Mike pretended to lose control of the car.

"We kept on just like that on and off for the hour or so ride to Salem," recalled Champagne, "going back and forth between joking and being serious. I knew I was going to Mexico and that was about it. I wanted a little adventure and a lot less aggravation. Mike gave me two grand in cash, reminded me of his pager number, insisted I keep in touch, and shook my hand. Then I climbed onto the Greyhound heading out of Salem. It was one hell of a long, boring ride. I bought a ticket all the way to Mexico City, but I knew I would have to get off before we crossed the border and do something about ID."

Phil did something about his ID.

"Back when I was a teenager it used to be that you could always dummy-up a fake driver's license from some other state and use it to buy beer or drive a car," explained Champagne. "That was back in the days before cops had all that computerized stuff or driver's licenses had holograms and fancy designs. You could just get some Letraset, a color photo, and with a little work and imagination, you could have an ID. Who the hell on the West Coast knew what a real Maryland or Rhode Island driver's license looked like anyway? You just made it up the way you thought it looked."

It had been more than thirty years since Phil had needed a false ID, so it took him a while to recollect the finer points of his creative adolescent endeavors. A

Polaroid camera, some smoked glass, rub-on lettering, and three days of trial and error in a border-town motel room resulted in Phil Champagne entering Mexico with a new name and driver's license to match.

"I called myself Peter Donovan," said Champagne with a shrug," and the driver's license really didn't look all that great. But it was good enough, because I didn't have any trouble getting across into Mexico and onto a crowded bus to Mexico City."

Whatever romantic illusions Phil Champagne nurtured about a clandestine crossing of Mexico's cordoned borders evaporated in the stifling heat of the overcrowded bus.

"My primary memory of that essentially unpleasant excursion was that every place we stopped, the toilets had overflowed."

He longed for air-conditioned comfort and an ice-cold drink.

Surrounded by strangers speaking an unfamiliar tongue, Phil closed his eyes and pictured himself aboard a powerboat slicing through glasslike water while refreshing spray splashed up from the sides of the bow. Fantasizing his way out of physical and emotional discomfort, he imagined a gentle breeze stirred the tree-lined shore and that he heard the clink of ice on glass, the splash of a jumping fish, and the sizzle of a thick, juicy steak.

THREE

The heaviest baggage for a traveler is an empty purse.
—German Proverb

"**H**arold Richard Stegeman was a high-rolling restaurateur who sold thick, juicy steaks and drove around Mason County in a fancy Cadillac," recalled *Shelton Journal* reporter Sean Hanlon. "He passed out hundred-dollar bills like they were candy and built a brand-new business from the ground up."

Terry Kinnaman, kitchen manager at Barb's Country Kitchen from October 1987 until February 1988, insisted that they served up the thickest, juiciest prime rib he had ever seen. Referring to Harold Stegeman, Kinnaman recounted the time his employer took Kinnaman and his wife, Linda, out to dinner at Miguel's restaurant in Tumwater, Washington. Stegeman moved his party to the head of the long line by softly snapping his fingers and slipping the maître d' a hundred-dollar bill.

"I was in awe because I'd never been around a person who could get other people down before him on their knees like that," Kinnaman said.

Despite the successful grand opening—Richard Fraley came in three times to sample the menu and offer congratulations—business at Barb's Country Kitchen began to decline. Harold was forced to sink the remainder of the wealth he had acquired for his retirement into the venture to keep it afloat. Good cooks and waitresses were rare in Shelton, and the service declined as the resources dwindled.

Barb placed the final classified advertisement in the *Shelton Journal* in June 1989. The bill for the ad was never paid, forcing the *Shelton Journal*'s bookkeeper, Donna Dooms, to turn Barb's Country Kitchen over for collection. In November 1989, Barb's Country Kitchen and Stegey's Blue Room were out of business.

Harold had borrowed on the restaurant, lost it, and was compelled to sell their home. Next, they sold their cars.

Seven separate liens and six tax warrants were placed against Barb's Country Kitchen between April 1989 and December 1990. The unpaid tax bills included $8,923.06 to the Internal Revenue Service, $6,300 to the Washington Department of Revenue, and $573.34 to the Washington Department of Labor and Industries.

Harold Stegeman filed for protection from his creditors under Chapter Eleven of the U.S. Bankruptcy Code, but the case remained unresolved because Harold, Barb, and the kids left town with a travel trailer and debts in excess of $200,000.

"We bought the travel trailer with the intent of moving back to Harold's old stomping grounds in Florida for a fresh start," recalled Barb with a sigh, "but my sister, Mary, fell ill and we went to Post Falls, Idaho, in February 1990 to offer whatever help we could."

They parked their trailer in Mary's yard and stayed for a month or so. Harold Richard Stegeman, a.k.a. Mr. Moneybags, had nothing left except his good name. Harold desperately needed to make money, and that meant taking whatever work was available.

The only work available to Phil Champagne in Mexico was whatever Mr. Smudge Collar's contact could arrange, but first Phil had to arrange accommodations.

"I got off the bus in what must be the world's largest bus terminal," recalled Champagne, "and the cab drivers were crawling all over me."

Vultures picking over freshly delivered carcasses may be a more accurate metaphor. Phil, the bumpkin gringo with no grasp of the language, was fresh meat.

The con ran smoother than the taxi: take the gringo to a third-class hotel with first-class prices, collect an outrageous fare from the passenger plus an appropriate kickback from the proprietor. If he didn't like the hotel, the driver got a second fare for taking him to another one.

"The first hotel was one step above a dump, and none of the staff could speak any English. It was what a travel brochure would term 'tiny colonial hideaway.' I had already paid the taxi driver, plus I tipped him, and then I had to hire him again to take me somewhere else."

The exchange rate was 159 pesos to the dollar, and Phil's second and acceptable hotel room in the Zona Rosa only set him back a respectable twenty-four dollars.

"And it was not a bad hotel at all," recalled Phil. "They had a first class bar jutting into the lobby off to the left as you walked in the door."

Bars held a certain fascination for Phil Champagne; he had always wanted one of his own.

Comfortably ensconced in his tourist hotel room, Phil Champagne steeled himself to make the phone call. He held the little book in his left hand for several minutes wondering exactly what the first words out of his mouth should be.

The first words should have been in Spanish.

"The person answering the phone didn't speak a word of English, and it didn't seem to matter how many times I said the name of the guy I wanted. I was about to give up when the man I was looking for came on the line."

Champagne had managed, over time and through trauma, to convince himself that his drinking buddy's recommendation would be sufficient reason for a total stranger to embrace him with convivial joviality and a firm offer of employment.

The subsequent chill almost froze the phone line. Phil had to explain, in elaborate detail, how and why he had the man's phone number. At length, the fellow gave Phil another man's name, a number to call, certain code phrases to use, and promptly hung up.

"It wasn't the reception I had anticipated, but as I did get a referral to another number, I was still hopeful."

Call number two yielded more encouragement. Although the contact had at first been reluctant to speak with him, Phil eventually swayed the voice at the other end of the line with his knowledge of prearranged codes. They agreed to meet in the first-class bar at the Zona Rosa.

Short dark, and obviously uncomfortable, Phil's first face-to-face contact contented himself with a cold beer while Phil attempted to make an excellent first impression.

"*Yo no comprendo*," said the man diffidently as Phil extolled the advantages of having a reliable gringo such as himself on the payroll. "I don't understand what it is you are talking about. You must have me confused with somebody else. However," the man added in an offhand manner, "I know a gentleman in Merida who might help you. Let me give you his name and number. You can tell him I told you to call."

Once again, Phil folded a napkin bearing information and stuffed it in his pocket.

The short, dark man tipped back the long-necked bottled, drained the last of his drink, banged the bottle firmly on the table, arose, and walked out. And just like the smoking beard in the battered blue pickup, he was gone without good-byes.

"Let's get the show on the road," Phil Champagne said to no one in particular and went upstairs to retrieve his belongings before checking out and hailing a taxi to the train depot.

"Before I left the hotel, I asked an English-speaking girl on staff how to say 'train today to Merida,' and she wrote it down for me on a piece of paper. She also wrote down other phrases I might find handy. She spelled them out phonetically so I could pronounce them."

"*Señor, un momento, por favor. Habla Ingles...,*" Phil said, trying his halting Spanish on the taxi driver stationed outside the hotel.

"Good afternoon, sir," replies the officious cabbie with mock formality, "my taxi and my command of the language are at your service."

"Now you're talking," said Phil enthusiastically as he hopped in. "To the train depot. I am on my merry way to Merida."

The cab driver shot Phil a bemused glance in the rearview mirror as they pulled out into the crazy Mexico City traffic.

"If you call a thirty-six hour train ride 'merry,' you will be very merry indeed."

Phil's merriment dissipated quickly.

"The cabbie took me to the train depot, let me off, and said, 'Be careful crossing the street. They will not stop for you.' He was right. I waited for a break in the traffic and ran across the street into a monstrous train station. It was gigantic, but there were hardly any people in it."

After decoding the schedule, Phil walked over to the ticket counter and recited the phrase provided by the girl in the hotel.

"*Merida, hoy.*"

"*No hoy, mañana,*" objected the expressionless ticket

master.

"*No, hoy,*" insisted Phil, knowing from the posted schedule that there was no reason for him to wait until the next day.

"*Mañana,*" deadpanned the man in the booth.

"*Hoy. Aquí, no amigos. Aquí, no dinero. Merida, amigos y dinero,*" explained Phil, citing neither friend nor money in Mexico City, but both awaiting him in Merida. He played his delivery and facial expression for sympathy. It worked.

"*Què lastima, lo siento mucho,*" the ticket master displayed a gap-toothed grin. "*Merida, hoy,*" he said, and allowed Champagne to purchase a ticket.

The train transporting the former Phil Champagne to the "Paris of the West" was manufactured in England and featured two special cars comprised of nine compartments each; less affluent passengers contented themselves on wooden day benches.

As Phil traveled to the cultural capital of the Yucatan, he decided to go first class—he brought along a bottle of vodka.

"I wound up sharing it with a funny little fellow in the compartment across from mine who kept making eyes at me. It turned out he was eager for conversation in English. He was a representative of John Deere, and the company had offered him a lucrative inducement to master the language. He had a Spanish/English dictionary; I had an English/Spanish dictionary. Between the two books and the bottle of vodka, we made the best of the trip."

Despite somewhat unwieldy urban inconveniences and a tragic history of subjugation and bloodshed, Merida is one of Mexico's most hospitable and nostalgic colonial cities. Following centuries of exploitation as slaves, the Mayans rebelled in the bloody Caste War of the 1840s. It is also Mexico's most important gateway for exploration of Mayan archaeology.

Phil Champagne was interested in neither archaeology nor nostalgia. He wanted an air-conditioned hotel room, and a positive response from his Merida connection.

Once in Merida, Phil boarded a beat-up bus with a blown muffler banging its way down the narrow streets to plop him off near the main plaza. The first hotel to catch Phil's eye was only nine dollars a day with no additional charge for the slowly turning interior fan. No thanks. He opted to pay three times as much up the street for air-conditioning, an English language radio station piped into the room, and a first class bar. No one seemed to mind that this affluent customer paid for everything with cash.

"No one can resist the appeal," said Champagne with a smile, "of a crisp, new hundred-dollar bill."

The famous portraits of Benjamin Franklin handed out by Phil Champagne in Mexico were 100-percent real. The bill tendered by Barbara LeHew Fraley at Señor Froggy's Mexican Restaurant in Spokane on October 15, 1991, was impressive, but fraudulent.

Assistant U.S. Prosecuting Attorney Tim Ohms appreciates a crisp, freshly printed Ben Franklin as much as the next guy, but the next guy wants a real one, too.

"It doesn't matter how pretty the bills look; if they are not real, they are not real. There is more to money than what it looks like or feels like," explained Ohms. "The ink is unique, as is the paper and the intaglio printing process."

Tim Ohms did not always speak with such confidence and unabashed self-assurance on matters regarding Federal Reserve Notes or issues of law and justice.

In the early 1980s, Timothy Ohms was a liberal arts under-graduate devoid of direction. By the joyous yuletide season of 1981, young Tim was in a panic. His college days were rapidly dwindling, and his future loomed as a vacuous financial uncertainty. His college transcripts verified his grasp of Greek literature, but employment prospects for Greek scholars were not among the bold type listings in the Help Wanted section of the *Tacoma News Tribune*. When it came to choosing a career, Timothy Ohms didn't have a clue.

Susa, Tim's older and wiser sister, grew weary of Tim's whining counterpoint to the intended atmosphere of holiday cheer.

"We have a law school right here in downtown Tacoma," growled Susan as only a loving sister can growl. "Be a lawyer and get a life."

Tim was astonished at her suggestion.

"It was like being struck in the head with a hammer," recalled Ohms. "I almost dropped my eggnog. The idea of law school had never occurred to me because I thought you had to do something like prelaw. I came out of a true liberal arts background and had never thought about law. In fact, I don't believe I thought about anything serious at all."

But eight months later in August 1982, Timothy Ohms was attending an orientation class at the Law Center of the University of Puget Sound on Pacific Avenue in downtown Tacoma, right next to the Greyhound bus depot and the dirty bookstores.

"I had visions of myself waiting tables at the Old Spaghetti Factory in downtown Seattle and going home at night hunched over a typewriter trying to write, if not the Great American Novel, at least something. So, I went to law school not out of any rational decision, but out of sheer animal panic," Tim shakes his head.

"I had no idea what I was in for. I was neither emotionally nor intellectually prepared for it," admitted Ohms. "I was in over my head."

On August 29, 1992, Phillip Wendell Champagne drove through downtown Tacoma, killing time before picking up Larry Wills at the nearby Sea-Tac Airport for the pre-Labor Day Weekend excursion in the San Juans.

"Had I known Tim Ohms back then, I would have parked the car, walked into the University of the Puget Sound Law Center, and invited him along," remarked Champagne.

Tim, overwhelmed by the implications of being a law student, would have been too burdened by homework to accept the invitation.

"When I got out of law school, I was still without direction. Things hadn't changed all that much. I still saw myself as Mr. Mediocrity. I jumped at the first job offered to me."

Tim Ohms' first job was working at a small law firm in Clarkston, Washington, located in the southeast corner of the state near the Idaho border. In a period of eight months, Tim didn't make a dime for his employers. He as happy to have the job but hungered for true court experience. When a job opened up as deputy prosecutor, Tim took the position.

"A year and a half after the superior court judge died, and as there are so few attorneys in Clarkston," Ohms said, "one of them was destined to be the new judge."

What Tim witnessed was neither a race nor a wrestling match, but, rather, a modified competition not unlike a beauty contest after which then-Governor booth Booth Gardner would award the appointment.

Shortly after the shifting of legal chairs and titles, the district court judge retired. Tim's boss in the prosecutor's office became district judge, and the position of Asotin County Prosecutor became vacant. Tim Ohms was the position's interim occupant.

"I thought to myself there is no way on earth that I could, or should, get this as a permanent position. But what the heck? Stranger things have happened. If I was going to be a lawyer, Asotin County Prosecutor was a job I would love."

In the six weeks before the county commissioners' final decision as to who would fill the position, Ohms hardly slept and seldom left the office. He was determined to demonstrate his unflagging determination and tireless dedication.

Just two years out of law school, Timothy Ohms was appointed Asotin County Prosecutor for the duration of the unexpired term or the next general election, whichever came first.

The election came first.

Going from door to door in suit and tie in the sizzling heat of an Asotin August, Tim Ohms campaigned to be elected to the office of Asotin County Prosecutor. He won.

"I figured that no matter what else happened in my life, I would always have this one great high point: Asotin County Prosecutor." Despite his attempts at self-deprecation, Ohms did an admirable job for Asotin County. In the early 1990s, his desire for new horizons prompted him to consider moving to China to teach English as a foreign language. A fresh job offer indefinitely delayed an excursion to the Great Wall.

On October 15, 1991, Timothy Ohms assumed his new position in Spokane, Washington, as assistant U.S. prosecutor. On his first day at work, Señor Froggy's Mexican Restaurant at 10521 East Sprague, reported receiving a counterfeit Federal Reserve Note in the denomination of one hundred dollars passed by a white female, later identified as Barbara LeHew Fraley.

The bogus bill was identical to those she had passed that same day at Spokane's Pioneer Pies, Frontier West Family Restaurant, and the HiCo convenience store. On November 6, 1991, she used an identical bill to pay for breakfast at Perkins Restaurant in Ritzville, Washington.

"The counterfeit bill passed by Fraley was very unique," commented Secret Service Agent Neil Goodman at the time of Barb's arrest. "It was a 1990 Federal Reserve Note—a new series of U.S. currency just released by the Treasury Department in an attempt to foil counterfeiters. The new bills have a vertical polyester thread between the edge of the bill and the Federal Reserve District Seal. It bears the initials 'USA' and the dollar denomination of the bill." Goodman said the counterfeit one hundred dollar bill seized in Ritzville was a 1990 series, but it did not have the polyester thread, which is invisible when the bill is held down on a flat surface. When held up to the light, the polyester thread is visible to the eye.

"This security enhancement," explained Treasury Secretary Nicholas Brady, "was added to one hundred dollar bills and will be added to other denominations because sophisticated color copy machines can duplicate almost exactly older Federal Reserve Notes in circulation."

Linda Bright, the Perkins Restaurant server to whom Barb had handed the hundred-dollar bill, didn't know about the enhanced security or the polyester thread. It never occurred to Mrs. Bright to hold up the bill to the light. If Linda's cash register had been adequately stocked with change, Barb, Harold, and Rich would have never been detained.

"The real irony," remarked Barb, as if it makes any difference, "is that I had no intention of using that hundred."

Could be. She had three other perfectly real ones in her possession at the time. All the other bogus bills were in Harold's pocket.

When Mrs. Bright failed to return, Barb's son, Richard Fraley Jr., became impatient and requested an explanation from a passing employee.

"The manager is having difficulty opening the safe. You will be helped shortly."

Rich offered to hasten the process by paying for breakfast with a smaller bill of his own.

"No, I don't have your ticket handy. Just be patient."

Having been in the restaurant business herself, Barb could not believe the poor quality of service.

"I know what it's like to be a waitress," asserted Barb. "I can't imagine how they could justify making us wait so long for our change."

FOUR

It is suicide to be abroad.

--Samuel Beckett

Sitting in the bar at the Zona Rosa in Merida, Phil Champagne, a.k.a. Peter Donovan, found the service and sustenance perfectly acceptable. All he awaited was the arrival of someone obviously looking for him.

The anticipated individual, for reasons purely intuitive, was easily espied. He was in his mid thirties, well shaved, medium build and height, nattily attired in a waist-length white cotton shirt with embroidered collar, and he trod on the cuffs of his too-long slacks.

Eye contact confirmed their appointment.

"My first impression was that the guy, Miguel, didn't trust me, and his English was not so hot. I figured I could win him over if I kept at it. In time, he seemed to change his attitude entirely."

First impressions are important.

Donovan recounted his years in the Merchant Marines, highlighted his excursion through the Panama Canal, and regaled Miguel with an animated retelling of the time *Foss LT377* barge, loaded with explosives from Hawaii, "escaped" to roam the mouth of the Columbia River.

To cover all potential employment bases, he put the final punctuation on his verbal resume by listing his accomplishments in the construction trade. Despite his apparent rudimentary grasp of English's more subtle shadings of expression, Mr. Nattily Dressed with the scuffed cuffs stretched his lips and showed his teeth. Peter Donovan interpreted the facial expression as a smile.

"*Comprende* sailboats?" asked Miguel.

"Sure, I know sailboats," confirmed Donovan. "I just came from an excursion on a forty-two-foot Westsail." Phil failed to mention that he was presumed drowned.

Miguel examined Peter Donovan as one would a midsized catfish before deciding whether to fillet it and grill it, or baste it and bake it.

"Cancun," said Miguel. "You know Cancun?"

Donovan shrugged. He had seen it on the map, knew it was supposed to be Mexico's tourist trap of the future, and heard it was a potential gold mine for builders.

"Miguel said he had a project under construction in Cancun and a sailboat there He wanted someone to move his sailboat and take on a few other jobs. As he was a man short, he said he figured he had just the right thing for a gringo like me. In fact, he said there was another gringo who also recently offered his services. He said we two gringos would be perfect for a few jobs in Cancun."

The mid-1980s building boom that vaulted Cancun into the global tourism arena had yet to ignite, and the Peter Donovan who traveled on Highway 180 from Merida to Cancun through Kantuil, Piste, the ruins at Chichen Itza, Valldolid, X-Can, and Puerto Juarez in Miguel's large, older, American sedan arrived in a relatively small and undiscovered resort bearing only the first scant fruits of preplanned glitz.

The two men checked into separate rooms at an inexpensive hotel in the City of Cancun. Miguel picked up the tab and informed Peter he had two days to play before the job began.

"No trouble," Miguel warns. "Don't get in trouble."

"*No problemo, amigo*," Donovan said with a grin, before promptly taking off to play tourist.

The city of Cancun was barely beginning to flex its muscle as a raffish boomtown, and the dashing Mr. Donovan was assuredly raffish. He sampled the restaurants and cocktail lounges, made friends with an Israeli businessman, and only moderately unnerved him by singing a German marching song.

"My musical selections were perhaps insensitive, but not ill-intentioned," remembered the aforementioned vocalist.

Donovan took a short sea-bound adventure to Isla Mujeres, a throwback to the days before Cancun ever existed, to explore a ruin of particular interest—the Mudaca Estate.

Fermin Mudaca, Donovan learned, was Isla Mujeres's most notorious pirate. After years of robbing and raiding, Mudaca retired and built a lavish estate to impress a local woman.

"And it still probably wasn't good enough for her," thought Peter, but then realized he may have been reading too much of his own experience into another man's history.

The mansion was in ruins, overrun by the jungle.

"Figures," said the tourist, and he returned to the newer constructions of Cancun.

"Over the next two days, more men came to see Miguel, but I couldn't tell what the hell they were talking about because none of them spoke any English, and Miguel spoke like Pancho on the old *The Cisco Kid* show. Finally, he tells me that I'm going to hook up with this other gringo and get to work. I figured it was about time."

The night before "work" was to begin, Phil attended an extravagant tequila party held at a home down a

Cancun side street at which he and the other gringo appeared to be the welcome guests of honor.

"The night was a blast. The food was great, and there were generous drinks and attractive señoritas. It was my first introduction to the other gringo, Sam. He was short and porky with one of those rough, red faces, and he couldn't seem to sit still for five seconds. He was always poppin' up and lookin' around. He reminded me of a hyper Pillsbury Dough Boy. As for the other guys, if they were up to anything crooked, they sure didn't look or act like it. Everyone was as nice as could be."

The following morning Miguel transported the gringos, who were hung over from tequila, down the south coast of the Caribbean Sea not far from Cancun.

A slight distance from a small village, a potholed blacktop road, its edges chipped away and sprouting weeds, gave way to a car-width swath of dirt and gravel trailing past shacks and down toward a concrete dock with a concrete bulkhead.

"It was barren and empty looking. All the trees were the same height, about twenty feet, and it was flatter than hell. When we pulled up, there was a van waiting with two guys in it. They didn't get out of the van, say hello, or anything. Considering that there was nothing going on except us, I thought it was peculiar. There were two boats in the water: a good-sized sailboat in front and an older wooden boat behind it."

In addition to the two unmovable strangers in the van, three other men waited in plain sight aboard the old wooden boat. As instructed, Phil and Sam loaded their personal items onto the sailboat, and then helped the three men move several weighty wrapped packages from the woodcraft to the sailboat. With that bit of manual labor completed, their snappy employer announced that he would pay the two gringos $100,000 to take the sailboat to Marathon, Florida.

Miguel promised to provide them with full instructions and directions. He asked Phil and Sam to wait for a moment on the wooden boat while he went to get them expense money for the trip. The three Hispanics followed along after Miguel.

"Sam seemed pleased and popped on over and sat down at the table aboard the wooden boat, but I was starting to get a giant knot in my stomach. For one thing, smooth Miguel suddenly spoke fluent English, which he sure didn't before. Also, I wondered why the three other Mexicans were tagging along after him if all he was going to do was get us some travel cash and come right back. I peeked to see what he was doing and where he was going. He went toward the van with the two guys in it, snapped his fingers, and motioned toward us with his thumb."

Mr. Nattily Dressed and his three shadows watched with detached businesslike interest as the two silent men emerged from the van and walked to an advantageous site on the concrete dock. They carried high-powered rifles. Phil Champagne, for the second time in the summer of '92, was in danger of death on the water.

Fear-powered adrenaline pumped violently through his system as he instinctively dove for cover.

"Get down and stay down!" Phil yelled in warning as he hit the floor.

Sam's response was to pop up.

CRACK!

The first shot blew off the side of Sam's head. Subsequent rounds came in rapid succession, blasting into the boat and showering Champagne with wood chips and splinters.

"There were fragments flying everywhere, stuff falling on me and hitting me from all directions. I remember thinking, 'How many in the clip?' 'How long can they shoot?' At least fifty to sixty rounds were fired into that old wooden boat, and there wasn't a damn thing I could do or a place I could go."

Champagne, blessed with an encyclopedic knowledge of firearms, made the parenthetical mental note that his assailants were using more modern weaponry than those with which he was personally familiar.

"I know they were more modern rifles because the high-powered rifles I'm familiar with make a hell of a noise, and these made a cracking noise. I figured they were using Chinese rifles with the super powder. You get almost the same ballistics," explained Champagne, "but without the noise."

Phil imagined that his immediate death was imminent. He only hoped it didn't hurt.

Silence.

"Then I heard doors slammin' and engines revvin' up and I thought, 'Jesus, they're not leaving, are they? If I've got a chance to run, I better take it.' I got up, and they were going back up the blacktop and coming up this dirt road from the side. Off in the direction of the little village comes this standard, dirty, Mexican police car. What they were doing there, I don't know. They weren't really coming too fast. There was a lot of dust as they headed off after the van and the sedan in what seemed to me a rather lukewarm pursuit. I could tell that they really didn't want to catch these guys if they were heavily armed with automatic weapons. They were just going through the motions."

Phil looked over at Sam and didn't enjoy what he saw.

"He had fallen sideways and slid under the table. He could have been hit three times for all I know, but I could see shit hanging from the side of his head. As I could see part of his brains, he was obviously dead."

Champagne scrambled from the bullet-riddled boat and boarded the sailboat to retrieve his travel bag.

"I could have grabbed one of those wrapped packages, but I didn't know what the hell was in 'em and I really didn't want anything to do with them. I just grabbed my bag and scooped up about forty or fifty dollars that Sam had in a little box on the sailboat. I knew Miguel and the boys would be back for those packages as soon as they could, assuming those packages were of any value, so I walked as fast as I could up the black top to the main road. From there, I could see the top of the hotels. It turned out I wasn't all that far from civilization."

Phil kept up a brisk power walk until he saw a little store by the side of the road.

"I bought a Carta Blanca beer. Later I figure out that it cost me sixteen cents. Then I told the kid in the store I wanted a goddamned taxi. Everyone understands 'taxi.' He got me one to take me into town, and then I hailed another one on the street and high-tailed it to the Cancun airport."

With frayed nerves and substantial motivation to vanish from Cancun, he began to swear in exasperation.

"A pilot came out from an office down the hall. He had heard me bitching, and he spoke English better than I did. He used my situation as an opportunity to show off. He asked me where I wanted to go, and I asked him what was available. His plane was leaving for Miami in forty minutes. The ticket cost me about seventy bucks, which I thought was reasonable, and despite my previous aversion to airplanes, I wasn't the least bit nervous when we taxied down the runway or takeoff."

Phil Champagne had once wanted adventure, but he didn't want it anymore. Mike was right; he had been out-classed by lowlifes. He had seen one man die that day, and Phil Champagne wanted to just get the hell out of Mexico and never, ever allow himself to be in a situation like that again. Peter swore he would never again play in Mr. McGregor's garden.

Rising above Cancun, leaving Miguel and a career in import/expert behind, Phil Champagne counted his blessings. The first four he thought of were his children. Turning his head away from the aisle, Phil Champagne quietly cried his way to Miami.

FIVE

Crime is as human as being charitable. Of course, we must have tribal laws. But crime...crime is like art, and the artist has always understood the criminal. The fear of the criminal is the same as the fear of the artist: both are terrified of exposure.

—Richard Lindner

Secret Service Special Agent Lyle Workman does not resemble Clint Eastwood, Bruce Willis, or Tommy Lee Jones. Lyle looks more akin to an effervescent Norman Fell topped with a dollop of Tom Arnold. Bouncy, energetic, optimistic, and blessed with a speed racer mind, in the fall of 1991, Workman occupied an office of organized chaos a few floors above Assistant U.S. Prosecutor Timothy Ohms in Spokane's Federal Building.

When Señor Froggy's found that perky employee Jeni O'Neil had innocently accepted a fraudulent one hundred dollar Federal Reserve Note, Lyle Workman got the call. After confirming the falsity of the Note, he attempted to find it in The Secret Service Big Book of Bogus Bills.

The size of a metropolitan telephone directory, the book lists every known counterfeit Federal Reserve Note passed in or out of the United States. Agent Workman wanted to know where the bill originated, how long the

Notes had existed, and whether it was an old Note still in circulation or a new one.

The counterfeit note passed at Señor Froggy's was not in the Big Book. Workman called headquarters.

"I wanted to know where it had come up in the United States before," Workman said, "so I asked myself, 'Do we have someone traveling through Spokane passing these, or is it the note itself that had made it to Spokane?'"

The answer was neither of the above.

"Bingo!" exclaimed Workman. "Lo and behold, they had no record of it either. Since the Secret Service is notified immediately when fraudulent currency is passed, I know the origin is Spokane as of that week. They could be made in Canada; they could be made in Texas, but we know the people who are passing them for the very first time are doing it in Spokane."

In a matter of days, identical notes poured into the Secret Service from Travis Carey at Pioneer Pies, David Davenport at Frontier West Restaurant, and David Nay at HiCo Exxon. O'Neil, Carey, and Davenport unanimously agreed it was a white female with short hair who passed the hundred dollar bills, serial number L44190499E. A notable exception was David Nay, cashier of HiCo Exxon convenience store. Nay remembered received the hundred-dollar bill but could not recall a single thing about the person who handed it to him. He did, however, recall absolutely everything about the person on whom he waited after receiving the hundred-dollar bill—Sharon Burgerson, an attractive nurse's aide who regularly patronized HiCo Exxon.

The attentive Mr. Nay, perhaps entranced by the customer's selfless dedication to the medical profession, even recalled the sundry nature of the nurse's purchases: a half-case of beer, five lottery tickets, and three packs of M&Ms.

"I have two kids," explained Ms. Burgerson, "so I

always grab a couple of M&Ms. The third pack was for me."

Strategically placed above the Twinkies, soda, and automotive lubricants, HiCo Exxon has video security cameras. While the recording quality is not broadcast standard, the resolution is often sufficient to identify suspected criminals. If Sharon Burgerson could be found on the videotape clutching a twelve-pack of Busch beer in one hand, and three packs of M&Ms in the other, Nay and Workman knew that the person preceding her was the passer.

Bingo!

Or almost Bingo.

The videotape revealed a white female with short hair preceding Ms. Burgerson to the cash register and proffering a hundred dollar bill at exactly 5:39 p.m. It also provided a black and white representation of the suspect's clothing, but her facial features were obscured.

"The whole issue was one of identification, not culpability," explained Tim Ohms. "Culpable means blameworthy. There wasn't any real question about her being the culprit, because here was the same individual going to four places in the same area, on the same afternoon, buying a pie with a hundred dollar bill, buying another pie from another store with another identical hundred dollar bill, and so on. It wouldn't be pie in the sky to assume the jury would conclude that this person is culpable. The only real question was, 'Who was this person?'"

Barb, Harold, and Richard's $18.73 breakfast at Perkins Restaurant in Ritzville, Washington, on November 6, 1991, suddenly made identification a more complex issue than Workman or Ohms had imagined.

While the young rich Fraley waxed impatient at Perkins, and Barb became increasingly nervous, Harold

Stegeman went for a walk.

"I could see trouble coming," acknowledged Stegeman. "I had a stack of counterfeit bills in my pocket, and I knew I had to get rid of them. When I saw Spike's Texaco about two-hundred feet away, I figured I had a good excuse to leave Perkins."

Harold Stegeman exited the restaurant and headed for Spike's while Barb and Richard waited for her change. On the way, he stepped over to a ditch and put the bills under a hunk of fresh sod by the telephone booth.

"With a little luck, Barb would appear to be an innocent victim."

Possibly, but it would take luck by the truckload.

"Innocent people do receive and pass counterfeit bills," confirmed Tim Ohms, "but they don't behave the way Barbara Fraley did. Even more important than Barb's nervous shaking, for which there could be an innocent medical explanation, was the fact that she left the restaurant without getting back the Note or receiving her change. If you're buying an eighteen-dollar breakfast and leave a hundred dollar bill, that's a pretty good tip."

According to Barb, she only went looking for Harold.

"Out the door I went," she said. "The manager, Todd Bright, followed after me with Rich one step behind him. They stopped on the walkway just outside the restaurant, but I continued across the parking lot toward the Texaco."

Barb, suddenly abandoned, became increasingly distraught. She walked around the Texaco, looking in windows for Harold. She couldn't find him anywhere.

"Assuming that she had criminal intent in passing this Note, she picked a lousy place to do it," commented Ohms. "It is one of the busiest Perkins in the world. Todd Bright, the manager, knows what real cash looks like. He recognized it immediately as counterfeit. He had the Note in one hand and the phone in the other when he called the Adams County Sheriff."

Todd Bright not only called the sheriff, he also called Perkins headquarters and reported the situation. He then redialed the sheriff's office to make sure law enforcement was on the way.

"If the Note had turned out to be real, Bright and Perkins would have been very embarrassed, and there might have been legal action against them by Barb. Todd Bright obviously had confidence in his judgment about the Note."

Barb's confidence in Harold as her knight in shining armor was by this time severely shaken. She had violated every rule painstakingly passed down by the all-knowing Harold Stegeman. Knowing he must be furious, she feared he had left her to her own meager devices, mounting panic, and a sense of impending doom.

Named for Phillip Ritz, a hardy homesteader who settled on acreage provided to him by the federal government in 1878, Ritzville is located along a lonely and isolated stretch of freeway that cuts across the high desert from east to west and connects the central and eastern parts of the state with Seattle. In the middle of the desert, Barb felt deserted. When the cops squealed into the parking lot, her extremities trembled with renewed vigor.

"She violated the rules, all right," Stegeman recalled with a laugh. "Rule number one: Never pass a bill when you are with the person holding the bundle. Rule number two: Never cash one when your car is around or your carrier is nearby. Rule number three: Only cash one where it is easy to disappear. And Rule number four: Never, ever try to pass a bill in the middle of the desert, especially at a place where they sell pancakes."

Ritzville Police Officer Ken Seuberlich and Adams County's John Hunt arrived in separate vehicles but were a united law enforcement presence for the pancake house scenario. Hunt stayed with Bright and Rich; Seuberlich went to retrieve wandering Barb, who had meandered aimlessly down the road toward a construction site.

Catching up with the ambulatory suspect, Seuberlich asked her what she was doing and where she was going.

Destinations at the I-90 off-ramp are limited, and unless Barb intended to crawl onto the freeway and stick her thumb out, there was no place to go except Spike's Texaco. No one could accuse Barb of attempting to flee— she arrived in her son's Subaru, and Rich was standing right next to Todd Bright the entire time.

"I'm looking for my husband," explained Barb.

"Where was your husband when you last saw him?"

"He was just here with us, but now I can't find him."

According to the authorities, Barbara LeHew Yokum Fraley then said the strangest thing.

"Well, I mean, my husband is at home, but I wish he were here."

Barb had now committed herself to searching for someone who could not be found because he was at home. Not smart. Not smart at all.

"That's not what I said," insists an exasperated Barb Fraley. "I said, 'He's here. He was here, but he's not here. I don't know where he is. My husband was here, but he's not my husband. I mean he's not my husband, but he is my husband. I've lived with him for almost six years, but I'm not married to him."

An understandable misunderstanding.

Seuberlich asked to see Barb's driver's license, but her intense shaking made it almost impossible to navigate the wallet out of her purse.

Todd Bright, Rich, and Officer Hunt joined the mid-street discussion. Bright informed Seuberlich that Barb and Rich were two of the three people dining together at Perkins.

"Where is the other man?" asked Seuberlich.

"There were just the two of us," answered Barb.

The breakfast ticket clearly showed three meals; Bright new three people had been served. Barb, not yet accused of any wrongdoing, appeared to be losing it.

"Nonsense," argued Barb. "I thought they asked me, 'How many of you were up at the till.' That's the reason I said that there were only two of us. Then they told me that the hundred-dollar bill was counterfeit and asked me where I got it. I told him I got it at Albertsons, the supermarket where I had cashed my check. He asked to see any other bills I had, so I showed them to him and he could see that they were real."

Barb and Rich were placed under arrest, read their rights, and cuffed and stuffed into the back of separate patrol cars. Harold Stegeman watched through the window of Spike's Texaco as Barb and Rich gesticulated in silence, and then evaporated in the desert.

Facing the situation head-on, Harold went to Spike's public phone situated next to the stacked cases of Bud Light and looked up the number of the Adams County Sheriff. Before he could make the call, officers walked through the door.

"I believe I'm the man you're looking for," offered the affable Mr. Stegeman. "I had breakfast with the two people who were just taken away, and I would like to know what exactly is going on."

As always, Harold was the essence of courtesy. He gladly showed them his impressive but fraudulent Cayman Islands resident permit and his authentic Florida driver's license. They took him to the sheriff's office for further questioning.

Lyle Workman did not meet Harold, Barb, and Rich until 1:45 p.m. Workman was busy conducting another counterfeit currency investigation in Idaho with Coeur d'Alene Police Detective Don Jaran when, at 11:45 a.m., he received a telephone call from Adams County Deputy Sergeant Mike Kline requesting Workman's response to

Ritzville to determine the genuineness of Barb's one-hundred dollar Federal Reserve Note.

"Call the state trooper," replied Workman. "Tell them I'm in my car, I've got one lousy blue light, and I am going to be going over the speed limit. I know we can hold the woman until we determine if she did this with intent or not, but the clock is ticking on what we can do with the two guys."

Lyle was also informed that the detained threesome was not being talkative. Barb had already called a lawyer, who advised her to remain silent, sign nothing, and do nothing.

"Right away, I'm thinking that this is the real McCoy," Workman said. "I've got the principals of the case in custody. So, I go bustin' butt out there with Special Agent Mick Mikalson. When we arrived, the officers filled us in on the details."

When the Adams County authorities pointed out Barb's cell, Workman walked over for a peek. Had it been a cartoon, his eyes would have sprung from their sockets with his jaw clanging noisily to the floor.

"I see exactly the same clothing on what appears to be the exact lady from the HiCo Exxon video! There is no doubt in my mind that I have the female who passed the Notes a month ago in Spokane. I should have confiscated her clothes as evidence, but didn't. Now I wonder, what else have I got? What else has the net dragged in?"

The next dragged in Harold Richard Stegeman.

"I take one look at this fellow, and he does look classy—blue blazer, khaki slacks, gold chain—and my first mental impression was, 'What is this guy doing here from Florida with this nondescript lady who, in my heart, I know is the lady who was in HiCo Exxon passing counterfeit money?' He was very nice, and I believe I detected a slight British accent, which only increased my astonishment at him being with these other two. The kid, a real wiseacre, looked like he belonged with Barb. But this guy? I mean, where did this ringer come from? I expected him to explain that he was some distant visiting relative or something."

Harold threw Lyle for a loop. Workman took a good look at Stegeman's identification.

"The Cayman Islands? Florida? Here's this guy who looks like Ronald Coleman, dresses to the nines, charming as possible, and I know he must be behind all this. In my twenty-five years with the Secret Service, I have never encountered a female counterfeit ringleader. I know the kid isn't the brains of the outfit, so that leaves Harold Stegeman. And I know I am going to have to let him and the kid go. Barb, I can keep, but those two are simply going to walk away. I know this is the guy, so I gotta be careful what I do with him. I could tell by his beginning comment that he, like Barb and the kid, was committed to not cooperating. They would cooperate as innocent victims of passing a Note, losing their minds, running, all that stuff, but not to the point where they would roll over and tell the truth."

Workman excused himself from Stegeman to speak with Barb.

"I'm not going to talk to anybody until I see an attorney," she stated flatly.

Lyle sat down, leaned over like an old pal, and spoke the truth.

"Here's my problem: I am entitled to fingerprints, photographs, and all other identifying information from any of you because that's a counterfeit hundred dollar bill. I have a right to get that, and then I can release anybody I think I can interview later. You know, Barb, I am definitely not going to be able to release you if you don't cooperate, because you're the one who tendered the bill."

Barb remained steadfast in her refusal to be

photographed or fingerprinted.

"You must make it easy," Workman told her as he left the cell to call Timothy Ohms.

"I knew I was going to have to set up an arraignment for her," Workman explained, "and in this district, you've got to do it as soon as possible."

When Tim Ohms took the call, Lyle Workman began his hyperkinetic retelling of the tale.

"I know right now, Tim, that we gotta bring this lady in. We have to get her arraigned today. I haven't talked to the kid yet, but he did give permission to search his car, which means there is nothing in it. The guy that I'm concerned about is Harold Stegeman. I want to get absolutely everything off his body and copy it. I have every right to know who he is because he was with her. As far as the son goes, we'll wing it."

"I'll start working on the magistrate thing right now," confirmed Ohms. "Call me back if anything changes."

While Special Agent Mikalson searched the suspect's Subaru, Workman took a short run at talking to Rich Jr. whom he apprised as a dedicated wiseacre and wannabe hard-ass.

Richard Fraley Jr., a tall, fine-featured and soft-spoken father of twins, admitted to an uncooperative attitude.

"Maybe I was supposed to be impressed that Workman had twenty-five years' experience with the Secret Service, but to me, he was just another cop," Fraley said. "I thought Mikalson was easier to deal with."

Lyle, rightly discerning that time spent with Rich was a poor investment, turned his attention to the dapper gentleman from the Cayman Islands.

"Listen, Mr. Stegeman," sighed Lyle, "if you are willing to cooperate, I need photographs and fingerprints. Show me everything that you've got to prove to me that you are who you are and that assures me that I can find you if I need to talk to you again, and you can be on your way. Does that sound okay?"

"Absolutely, Mr. Workman," agreed Harold. "I'll do whatever I can to help."

Lyle brought him out to the printing area, and while his prints were taken, the two men engaged in an approximation of relevant small talk.

"He was the nicest guy in the world," said Workman. "I told him that Barb should be much more cooperative, and he said that she had a tough life. I mean, he would make some excuses for her but not try to fill in what happened, which told me again that he was in control. He was willing to hand her up, willing to let her sit there, but he was not about to start making up stories about how she got the counterfeit bill."

Harold posed for photographs while Lyle searched Harold's wallet.

"Everything was in place," Workman said. "Then I pulled out a business card from the money part of Stegeman's wallet: Inland Photo Supply. I flipped it over and, BAM! LIGHTNING BOLTS! BELLS! DING-DONG. DING-DONG! THIS IS IT! On the back of the card is the following: arcing light, photo plates, bond paper, opaquing equipment. Here are the ingredients for counterfeiting handwritten on the back of the card. Well, I'm not going to let him see my reaction. Internally I'm going nuts, but not on the outside. I don't give it away."

A few moments later, Adams County officers brought Workman a computer printout of the trio's criminal records. Little Rich had one Failure to Appear, Barb had her old forgery charge, and Harold R. Stegeman of 6822-22nd Avenue North, Apartment 106, St. Petersburg, Florida, was clean as a whistle.

Attached to the short report was a longer, more interesting addendum: the extensive Florida criminal history of Ronald Edsel Kollister, alias Harold Richard

Stegeman.

Kollister, a familiar and unpleasant face to the Metro Dade Police Department, was busted on January 19, 1984, for possession of cocaine with intent to sell and placed on probation. Charged with the same offense four months later, he was not prosecuted. The printout read, "released to another agency." Two months later, the same play was acted out again. The arrest and release record of Ron Kollister kept a steady pace until his sudden disappearance in late 1985. In America's War on Drugs, Ron Kollister was apparently a double agent.

"Kollister was a real guy, and that was his real name," explained Workman. "He had been arrested and put into the system. I would surmise from the pattern that he may have been working undercover for the DEA. Obviously, at some time in his criminal career, he used the name Harold R. Stegeman. Was our Harold R. Stegeman really Ron Kollister? The two men had different Social Security numbers and different descriptions. I wanted to know who the hell this guy really was, where he came from, and what in the world he was up to."

Despite the identification conundrum and the revelatory contents of Stegeman's wallet, Lyle had no legal reason to hold Harold and Rich. Barb, still refusing to be photographed, stayed behind bars while awaiting transfer to Spokane. The next day, November 7, 1991, the United States of America filed criminal complaint 91-0266A-01 charging Barb with violation of Title Eighteen, United States Code, Section 472.

"I was afraid that I would never see Harold again," admitted Barb. "I imagined that he would simply vanish or take off back to Florida."

The thought occurred to him, but Phil never seriously considered it.

"I couldn't turn my back on her like that," insisted

Harold. "Besides, I knew it was only a matter of time until they came for me, too. As for Florida, I didn't know what would be waiting for me there."

Phil Champagne breezed his way through United States Customs at the Miami airport, honestly answering "Seattle" as his place of birth.

"It's a good thing I didn't lift any of those packages from the boat in Cancun. After I went through customs, I was asked if I minded being sniffed by a drug dog. The dog sniffed, and I walked away."

A few humid days in Miami's unique sociological atmosphere prompted Champagne to seek another destination.

"Miami is loaded with riffraff in general. There were blacks fighting Hispanics, violence everywhere, and I am just not into that sort of lifestyle, if you can call it a lifestyle."

The image of Sam's brainless head was fresh in his mind, serving as sufficient motivation to jump a bus for Tampa. Once off the Greyhound, Phil Champagne, still calling himself Peter Donovan, checked into an inexpensive downtown hotel within walking distance of the bus depot.

"I think they were going to tear it down, and I bet they have by now. I only stayed there one night, picked up a newspaper, and began looking at apartments for rent. I still had a little bit of money, but it had to be something cheap."

Armed with a newspaper and basic curiosity, Phil Champagne set out to see the sights of daytime Tampa and ended up on a street with no high-rises but "every restaurant known to man on it. Name a chain and one of the links was on this street. I went into a service station and asked if I could toss my travel bag up on one of the shelves while I wandered around, and they were real nice about it. I didn't know what the hell I was doing, or where I was going to wind up. Then I saw the ad in the paper for the guy with the trailer."

The guy with the trailer was an American war veteran with cancer of the larynx who wanted a roommate who might also be his friend. Standing at a restaurant pay phone, Phil Champagne answered all the important questions: "How old are you? And 'Are you gay?'"

Phil was momentarily discouraged by the reference to sexual preference.

"No, I'm not gay."

"Good. Neither am I."

"How do I get there?"

"I'll come get you."

Despite his recollection of directions and dialogue, Champagne has two handicaps: he is dreadful with names, and he can't spell.

"He had a very common name, but damned if I can recall it. I remember his last name was Polish but sounded Italian. I do remember that we went out to his mother's house in Brooksville. She had a nice house on the golf course. We stayed overnight and swam in her pool.

"He really wanted to keep me as a buddy because he didn't have any. Mostly, he wanted to find himself a woman. He knew where they were but was not adept at meeting, greeting, and conquest. It was his idea that we go to a singles' dance. Not as a couple, of course," Phil clarifies, "but in search of women."

With less than a week of Tampa under his belt, Peter Donovan was about to move uptown, alter his lifestyle, and discover he was blessed with a talent far beyond building cost-efficient condominiums. Peter Donovan had a way with women.

High atop a Tampa motel, it was ladies' choice at the singles' dance when he sauntered in the door. Before he could sit down, Peter was dragged willingly onto the dance floor. After five or six minutes of backbeat gyrations, he relaxed with liquid refreshment and romantic inclinations with dark-haired Ann of forty-seven years, slender build, and swollen bank account. They talked, flirted, and toyed with each other's emotions. He swept her off her feet; she scooped him up and took him home.

A self-supporting woman of sufficient backing, Ann would neither invest her libidinous urges in a one-night stand, nor take umbrage at Peter's two-week reluctance at becoming a well-kept man.

"When she first asked me to move in with her, I wouldn't do it. But then I thought, 'What the hell? It's better than living with this guy in a trailer court off Elrod Avenue, even if it is air-conditioned.'"

Eight months later, Ann and Peter were still an item.

"I told her that I was a former real estate developer from the West Coast who had lost everything in a messy divorce, which wasn't so far from the truth. Her late husband had been an Air Force colonel who had left one hell of an insurance policy in addition to his military insurance. Her father had died some years before and left her property, which she sold for about half a million dollars. She was always buying stocks and bonds and showering me with gifts. The elaborate gifts took a while to get used to, but I adjusted. She had a delightful house just off West Shore Boulevard on the peninsula halfway between Gandy Boulevard and Kennedy Boulevard. I made myself useful by building her a new patio, gazebo, and doing other constructive work around the house."

Not wanting her beau embarrassed by lack of funds, Ann insisted he open his own bank account in which she placed thirty thousand dollars.

"When we started the account, I made sure it was non-interest bearing. That way, I wouldn't have to worry about any problems with taxes or a double-check of my Social Security number." While Phil/Peter improved the physical and romantic atmosphere of Ann's domicile, he also improved the quality of his bogus identification.

"The more I made, the better I got at it. I made plenty of it right there in her house, but she never knew it. I simply made IDs that would back up even more who it was I claimed to be. She was wonderful to me, and I didn't want anything about me to appear suspicious."

As time went by, Ann's gifts became more expensive and increasingly lavish. Phil began feeling both guilty and possessed. He tried refusing her gifts, but that only seemed to offend her.

"Being on the receiving end of a woman's generosity must have been a unique experience for Phil," commented John Robin. "He was always the provider, the one coming up with what it took to take care of things. I can't imagine Phil feeling good about himself in a situation like that."

He didn't except when he made valid contributions to either the quality of her life, or the size of her bank balance.

During an afternoon visit to Ann's stockbroker, Peter earned her respect as a trusted financial advisor when he rebuked the man for charging her a fee.

"Ann, do you mean to tell me that you're the purchaser of these bonds, and you have to pay him a commission? The seller pays the commission, Ann, not the purchaser. This is bullshit."

The broker's objection never escaped his lips.

"Bullshit," reiterated Mr. Donovan, now turning his attention to the broker. "That's bullshit for you to charge her two percent on that. Why should she pay you two thousand bucks?"

Rather than appear argumentative, the broker made appropriate adjustments in Ann's favor.

"They do get you on both ends in those deals," notes Champagne, "except if you bitch about it, then they let it go. Well, Ann was real impressed that I bitched. It saved her two-thousand dollars and bought me more than that in credibility and admiration." Ann also bought him a boat. Not a rowboat, not a little powerboat, but a forty-five foot trawler valued at a hundred-and-fifty thousand dollars."

"At first I was furious," said Phil with a shrug, "but, once again, I accepted the gift. When we finally parted as friends, I went to her lawyer and explained that I still had thirty thousand dollars of hers in my bank account, plus title to this rather extravagant trawler. I didn't want anybody to ever say I stole it or conned her out of it or anything that could get me in trouble. He checked with her on the telephone right there and then. She confirmed that she wanted me to keep the money and the boat. Well, I wrote her a check for the thirty grand and left it with him. The deal was this: If in thirty days she was still refusing to take the check, he would tear it up and the money was mine, free and clear. Thirty days later, he tore up the check."

With $30,000 in his bank account, and a forty-five foot trawler beneath him, Peter Donovan took off down the inland waterway to the Florida coast via Lake Okeechobee.

"The stupidest damn thing I ever did," insisted Phil Champagne, "was trying to navigate those damn canals at night, drunk. Hell, I could have died out there on the water."

Again.

"You don't have to be much of a sailor just to follow the markers and look on your chart."

But Phil lost the markers, couldn't focus on a chart, and found himself in shallow water and high grass in the middle of the night. Champagne turned on his searchlight, scanned the water, and finally discerned the route out.

"Sounds like the story of my life," commented Champagne. "Every time I would get in a situation like that I would pray to God and say, 'I'll never do anything stupid like this again,' and then, sooner or later, I would be right back in the same kind of trouble. Sometimes, like with that damn restaurant, Barb's Country kitchen, I was too proud to see that I was gonna drown."

SIX

My problem lies in reconciling my gross habits with my net income.

—Errol Flynn

Barb and Harold viewed the situation as hopeless. Even when Harold entered severe depression, which was infrequent, he didn't seriously blame anyone except himself.

"I should have known better, but I didn't know anything about the restaurant business. The restaurant was fine; it was the location." Harold suddenly brightened. "Let's blame your sister Mary."

Barb gave him a look, lit another white-tipped filter cigarette, and tossed the tattered matchstick into the motel-style ashtray in the corner of the trailer's imitation kitchen table.

"Good idea, honey. Let's just walk right up to Mary and say, 'You know, it's all your fault for talking us into building twenty miles away from where any sane person would go for dinner.' Yes, Mary will certainly appreciate that."

"Hmm…" For the first time in a long time, Harold Stegeman smiled. "Yeah, I'll storm right up to her sickbed, stamp my foot, and yell at her about how Shelton is nothing but drug dealers, mushroom pickers, and welfare mothers." Harold and Barb, making light of the absence of such at the end of their interminable tunnel, laughed until tears cued their true emotions.

"You can't get help," said Barb flatly, referring to the incompetence of waitresses.

"Yeah, the help just brought us down."

"The biggest mistake made was not shutting down four months after we opened. I should've shut down right then on the spot. I could have said, 'Oops, let's make this into a house. We'll live in it—anything. But I didn't want to admit defeat, and I kept thinking, 'We'll do this, we'll do that.' Bullshit."

Barb, who had been holding her breath, exhaled.

"We had the customers. We had people sitting on logs outside waiting to get in."

"And the food was good. The prices were right."

"It was thirty-six hundred square feet, and we could have lived in it if we had sold the house. Hell, we could have closed down the restaurant and lived in the damn thing."

The cigarette broke above the filter as Barb stubbed the tip into the ashtray. She shook her head in negative agreement as Harold continued.

"We could have closed the doors and still had two-hundred thousand dollars left over in the bank."

If only, should have, could have—the litany of loss, the chorus of discontent.

Harold and Barb discussed a variety of ventures before building the restaurant. They considered pizza by the slice in the mall, a dry cleaning operation, and several franchise businesses.

"The entire idea," explained Harold, "was for us not to have to work. We make the investment, build it up, hired a good manager, and enjoy ourselves."

It didn't work that way.

"I ended up working six days a week, seven days a week," Barb recalled, "and that got real old, real fast. We took the breakfast shit out and turned the place into a dinner house with lanterns on the table and curtains on the windows. When we first opened up, folks came from near and far for a taste of our prime rib."

They came from as far away as Gresham, Oregon.

Don Robertson, attorney for diverse members of the Champagne clan, stopped by Barb's Country Kitchen with his wife and friends after a weekend of sailing off the Washington coast.

"I'd heard the story about how a former waitress named Barb had a wealthy boyfriend build her this restaurant," explained Robertson. "My friend was showing me around the bar while my wife, Bobby, waited for our table. I walked in, looked around, and saw a man standing there who looked exactly like my old friend and client, Phil Champagne. As I went to approach him, he turned on his heels and went into a back office. When I returned to Bobbi, she said I looked as if I had seen a ghost. I told her I believed I had."

The apparition may have been Mr. Moneybags to the locals, but he was Mr. Useless around the restaurant.

"I could see that he couldn't tend bar and he couldn't cook or wait tables. He could do dishes, but I needed to have more help than that," said Barb. "So, I showed him how to do the books. I had an accountant, but you still have the books, and you still have inventory, and things like that. The idea was for Harold to take over the paperwork so I could concentrate on everything else."

In charge of the books and paying the bills, Harold perceived negative cash flow and financial ruin creeping across the ledger.

"Barb didn't want to face the restaurant's financial difficulties," commented Stegeman. "I tried to tell her many times that the place was going down the tubes, but she didn't want to talk about it. If I started to tell her what was happening financially, she would walk off. I wanted her opinion about what to do, and she said it was up to me. She was working hard night and day to make a go of the restaurant, so I paid the bills in full as long as possible. But when the money wasn't there, I had to decide who got paid first."

Harold made an appointment with the tax people to arrange an extension and devise a new payment schedule. He was promptly advised that he had no right to use collected sales tax for any purpose other than paying sales tax.

"You've got people standing there that need their pay to support their families," protested Harold. "There is not enough to pay both them and the tax. Who am I going to pay first? I'll tell you: I'm going to pay the person who needs the money to feed their family and pay their bills. That's why I'm here trying to work something out with you. Would you rather I paid the taxes and didn't pay my employees?"

No employee of Barb's Country Kitchen ever went home without every cent they had coming; no one who worked for Harold Stegeman could ever say the man didn't take care of them.

Barb may have been tempted to throttle Harold for allowing his ethics to propel them to bankruptcy, but Harold's beloved has a forgiving nature.

"When this happened, I felt like I owed him anyway," Barb said. "In fact, I wanted to make the restaurant work so that I could pay him back for everything he had done for us. I never had to worry about money. He would give me money anytime I wanted it. If one of my kids needed a pair of shoes, he was there to buy it. If one of the boys wanted a car, he would buy him a car. When the younger boy wanted a motor dirt bike, Harold bought him the dirt bike. If I needed something, it was there."

When the payroll taxes needed to be paid, it wasn't there. When the sales tax needed to be paid, it wasn't there. Soon, Harold and Barb were not there either.

SEVEN

A man who has money may be anxious, depressed, frustrated and unhappy, but one thing he's not and that's broke

—Brendan Francis

With the ill-fated restaurant reduced to the topic of regretful conversation, Harold and Barb surveyed the future's possibilities from their vantage point of depression. Their future, it appeared, was all used up.

They headed south to visit Barb's sister in Roseburg, Oregon, for a few days, and then traveled down to Reno, Nevada, to see her brother who earned his money painting Jackpot Food Marts for Time Oil. A phone conversation with her sister Mary turned Harold and Barb back toward the Northwest.

"Mary was going in for exploratory cancer surgery in Post Falls, Idaho. She was scared and I was worried for her. She asked me to please come and be with her, so I did. We parked our travel trailer in her yard and stayed for about a month before we rented a small house."

Barb found immediate employment at Conoco Port Truck Stop as a cook; Harold bounced from industrial painting to a position as shipping supervisor for red Label Express. After a year of cooking and shipping, the two were offered positions at a wood manufacturing plant. Harold declined, but Barb accepted.

BURL BARER

"I was promised a lot more money than what I was making as a cook. I was told I could make as much as thirty-three thousand a year. I had only been working there a week when I lost half of my little finger in an industrial accident. I was on L&I for nine months and received a small compensation check for the loss of my finger."

The compensation was $720 a month until her hand was healed, followed by a $2,500 final payment.

Harold had all his fingers but no pies to put them in. The shipping job was employment without destination. Overworked and underpaid, he quit. Stegeman no longer drove a fancy car, nor did he hand out hundred dollar bills like they were candy. Time was not on his side, his head was in his hands, and his beer was lukewarm. So much for being an entrepreneur. It is hard to be a capitalist without capital. Harold Stegeman arrived in Shelton with over $300,000. He had been, in every sense of the word, a self-made man. If self-worth were measured in denominations of negotiable currency, Harold Richard Stegeman had become worthless.

"Becoming a criminal was essentially an executive decision based on financial need," explained Stegeman. "I had to decide exactly what kind of criminal I was going to be. I knew I wasn't going to stick up a bank, because I don't have the guts, and I'm not violent. I refuse to do anything that's gonna hurt an individual. I hate to say this about myself, because nobody believes it, but if I saw a workingman drop his wallet and it had $700 in it, I would be the first to see that he got it back. I would not destroy someone under any circumstances."

Harold mentally listed crimes with profit potential, ruling out armed robbery or elaborate cons.

"Never forget," cautioned Secret Service Agent Neil Goodman, "that he is a swindler and a convicted felon."

Harold was technically neither when he chose his

criminal career.

"Swindler? If I was going to swindle old people, I wouldn't take their old-age money. Now, if an old lady has three hundred thousand in the bank, I might take three thousand of it because that is not going to make a hell of a lot of difference. The idea would be to take a small amount from each person and let it add up. Never take a lot from one person. That should be the rule."

True criminals seldom draft rules of conduct, and Harold hadn't juggled this many justifications since Anacortes in '82.

"Counterfeiting," ruminated Stegeman. "What would that hurt? Even if a shopkeeper dropped a hundred dollars here or there, it wouldn't close him down. And he could probably pass it on to the next person, and they had the option to either turn it in or pass it on. I figured that counterfeiting was the one crime least likely to hurt anybody, and it never entered my mind that I couldn't do it."

Harold began his education with a simple trip to the library in Coeur d'Alene, Idaho. He read a few books; he figured it out.

"I looked up lithography, studied some diagrams, and saw that it was a very simple thing to do. I could give anybody ten hours of instruction and they could do it as well as I did. I figured out my own method, and I went ahead and did it. I was fairly pleased with what I got."

He got twenty-one months.

"The idea was not to counterfeit for a living, but only to generate enough to have a nest egg to start something legit. I didn't realize how difficult it would be to pass enough to have that nest egg."

It is one thing to read about counterfeiting; it is quite another to actually print bogus bills.

"I know a lot of these Secret Service and FBI guys that say that counterfeiting is the last crime you would ever want to get involved in, because every time you cash one, you're sticking your neck out—committing crime after crime, where you eventually gotta get caught."

It was Barb's neck that Stegeman kept sticking out.

"Yeah, well, I do have to take responsibility. But then again," said Harold with an honest smile, "I'm not the one who broke the rules."

Rules are important to authoritarians and game players. "At first it was as easy as a Frontier Pie," quipped Harold. "I drove Barb around, and she cashed them one right after another. Somewhere between 4:00 and 5:00 in the afternoon on October 15, we decided to go to Spokane, came down Sprague Street heading west, and stopped at the first business that looked like they could handle it. We just went on right down the line. I remember hitting fast food places and a pie place."

David Davenport of Frontier West Restaurant and Bakery vividly remembered his encounter with the woman who handed him a counterfeit hundred-dollar bill sometime after 8:00 p.m. on October 15.

"I told her that our Pie of the Month was strawberry-rhubarb. She said that she would take one, so I boxed it for her. She said that she was sorry, but all she had was a hundred dollar bill. I took the bill and gave her change, and then she left the store. From the time she walked into the building until she left, she was there five minutes at the most."

By the time Davenport realized the bill was bogus, the woman with the strawberry-rhubarb pie was gone.

"I don't like rhubarb," Barb testified ruefully. "I have never liked rhubarb. My kids don't even like rhubarb. I would not purchase a rhubarb pie for any reason."

Lyle Workman always wondered about the pies.

"What did they do with those darn pies? I thought maybe if we had gone out in back of the Frontier Restaurant, or Pioneer Pies, we would have found perfectly good strawberry-rhubarb pies, still in their boxes, tossed in the Dumpster."

"No," clarified Harold Stegeman, "we just tossed all those pies and stuff in the back of the van and kept driving. We cashed twenty-one bills that night. It could have been twenty-two, but I think it was twenty-one, because it was new to us, and we were keeping pretty close track."

Fond memories make for grandiose minimizing. From initial concept to hard currency realization, the project was fraught with failures, falsehoods, and fear. And contrary to early assumptions of the Secret Service, no great thought went into Stegeman's selection of the 1990 Federal Reserve Note as the pattern for his counterfeiting efforts.

"There was no master plan, no flash of creative insight," explained Harold. "In fact, I was sitting in a coffee shop with Barb's nephew, Monte LeHew Jr., when I noticed he had a new looking bill. I asked if I could borrow it for a day or two. I took a picture of it and gave it back."

As for the security fiber found in real 1990 Federal Reserve Notes, Harold had never heard of it. He knew about the red-and-blue threads found in authentic currency, but he simply chose to ignore them.

"You must remember that I was working with a very small budget on this project, was not using the latest technology, had never attempted this before, and was learning as I went along. After all, if I had been able to go high-tech, I could have afforded to do something legal."

Lyle Workman, well acquainted with the finest efforts of professional counterfeiters, was amazed at the quality of Harold's barnyard operation.

"What this guy did, the way he approached it, was like something out of the 1930s or '40s," Workman said. "It was the ultimate in old-fashioned, low-technology counterfeiting."

"That's me, all right," acknowledged Harold, "old-fashioned and low-technology. I only went to eighth grade, and I have no idea what my IQ is."

Tested in elementary school, he scored ninety-four in the first grade and eighty-five in the second grade. That was back in the 1930s.

"Forget those old IQ tests," insists Lyle Workman. "There is no doubt that he really is one hell of a bright guy with a remarkable amount of ingenuity. He probably could be anyone he wanted to be if given the opportunity."

On the Florida coast in the 1980s, he wanted to be Peter Donovan, a dapper mariner remembered for his generosity at the bars and his ability to belt out marching songs in impressive German.

"Phil always could do a great German accents," recalled John Robin. "We used to pull that stunt all the time. We would go into cocktail lounges and pretend that we were German tourists or German sailors. I was married to a German girl for quite a while, so I knew the language. Phil just had a natural talent for imitating accents and mannerisms. When he got a few drinks in him, Phil would launch into those German songs. I'm not the least bit surprised to hear that he was doing the same thing wherever he went, whatever name he was using."

At long last, with money in the bank and a beautiful boat of his own, it was a wonderful life.

Phil Champagne had everything he needed, including an excellent set of fraudulent identification.

EIGHT

How hard it is to escape from places. However carefully one goes they hold you—you leave little bits of yourself fluttering on the fences—little rags and shreds of your very life.

—Katherine Mansfield

The papers were forgeries that authorized three-year-old Peter Richter to travel unhindered from Czechoslovakia to the British sector of West Berlin in 1947.

"My coat lining and the soles of my shoes contained the few precious stones and what money my parents could call their own," recalled Richter. "My father was in the French underground during the war, joined the British army, and arranged the false papers for mother and I. Two drunken American GIs met us at the end of the line. I remember that they drove so fast, I could hardly breathe."

Richter and his parents survived Hitler's assault, but his grandmother and aunts were less fortunate.

"My grandmother was Jewish," related Richter, "and when the Germans invaded Czechoslovakia, they started rounding up the Jews and sending them to the death camps. Grandmother and father's two sisters were about to embark on a boat for South America when the Nazis came on board. They grabbed my grandmother and one of the girls, but a gentile woman grabbed the other one and insisted that the child was hers. "She doesn't go with the Jew,' she said. So my grandmother and the one child died in the concentration camp, and the other child was raised in San Paulo, Brazil, by the woman who saved her life."

The Richters left West Germany for America, making their new home in Yakima, Washington. They moved to Lake Oswego, Oregon, in 1950. Graduating in 1962 from the University of Oregon, he decided to take a sentimental journey back to Czechoslovakia.

"When I applied for my visa, I discovered that I was still considered a Czech citizen. It was quite likely that I would be conscripted into the Czech army. Instead of taking the trip, I bought a motorcycle."

Richter passed the Oregon bar in 1971, joined the law firm of Miller, Nash, Wiener, Hager, & Carlson in 1973 and became a partner in 1978. Despite an understandable lack of appreciation for strident German marching songs, he has, as legal counsel for Federal Kemper, been directly linked with the strange case of Phil Champagne since Mitch first filed his claim for the $1.5 million insurance policy.

"My first involvement was June 10, 1983. I received a telephone call from an in-house lawyer with Federal Kemper. Mitch Champagne had filed suit to collect, and this fellow wanted me to look at the case. He sent over an Equifax investigative file about eight inches thick."

The agreement and release reached between Federal Kemper Life Assurance Company and William M. Champagne on November 7, 1083, stipulated that $700,000 would be paid to Champagne's attorney, John L. Hilts, who was to deduct his reasonable attorney fees and immediately pay Champagne one-fourth of the balance. The remaining funds were to be held in trust and paid out in fourths, every three months, until the full sum was paid.

The signed agreement specifically stated: "Payment by Company hereunder is expressly conditioned on the assumption that the insured is deceased and claimant agrees that, if at any time, the insured reappears or is found alive, claimant will forthwith reimburse Company all sums paid hereunder, less Hilts' attorney fees."

When Phil came back from the dead, Richter was back on the case.

"Once again I received a telephone call from an in-house lawyer for Federal Kemper. They no longer had the paperwork related to the original claim, and their computer only told them that they had paid out six thousand dollars. I advised them that Kemper had paid out a more significant sum."

Kemper filed suit against Mitch, Phil, and little brother John Robin.

"We don't make any claims of fraud against Mitch for two very good reasons: There is no hard evidence of any kind linking Mitch with any attempt to defraud the insurance company; the clear situation with the stipulation in the original settlement which basically said that if Phil ever turned up alive, Mitch would have to pay the money back. Phil is alive; pay us back."

Kemper, however, accused Phil and John Robin of conspiring to defraud the insurance company.

"This not a criminal case, but an insurance matter," clarified Richter. "Essentially, we are taking about financial obligations."

When news of Kemper's suit reached John Robin, the pain stung as the assault of a serpent.

"First I lost my brother, then Renee accused me of murdering him, then I was sued by Joanne who claimed I was responsible for Phil's death, and now they say I helped Phil fake his death so that Mitch could collect the insurance," moaned an incredulous John Robin. "What could I have possibly gained from Phil's death, be it real or otherwise? All I've reaped is anguish, tears, and lawsuits. Why would anyone accuse me of such things?"

Ask Peter Richter.

"Well, it makes sense to seek a default judgment against Phil because he didn't let us know he wasn't dead. The circumstances of Phil's alleged death are such that if Phil faked it, John Robin probably knew about it."

As for what John Robin was supposed to get out of the alleged insurance fraud, Kemper and Richter have no idea. Investigations show that he had no sudden influx of money following Kemper's payment to Mitch.

A careful check was also made of the financial condition, credit rating, and recent travel history of Marianne Hauser, a talented and successful real estate agent who had become a close friend of Phil in the months before his watery demise. The German-born Hauser, a former ballerina noted for her integrity and business savvy, was the ex-wife of Gresham's Robert L. Hauser. They were divorced on April 30, 1973. The investigation revealed Marianne Hauser had no financial difficulties and an A-one credit rating. If there was a list of likely suspects in a case of potential insurance fraud, Hauser was off the list.

Larry Wills, also subject to careful scrutiny, was on the boat when Phil disappeared, but Federal Kemper made no allegations against him. For the record, Wills's version of what happened August 31, 1982, is the same as John Robin's. When a thorough investigation of Wills's financial situation was conducted on behalf of the insurance company, nothing even remotely suspicious was uncovered. A primary question Kemper had about Mr. Wills was simply this: "Why had Phillip called him after so long a time to go on a fishing trip?"

It wasn't Phillip who had called, explained Larry. It was Mitch. The two men had lost track of each other for many years after their school days, but their friendship was rekindled in the later 1960s when Mitch tracked him down to repay a $200 debt he had owed Wills for over twenty years. Larry Wills and Mitch Champagne saw each other once or twice a year, every year, ever since. Mitch would go to Boise to hunt with Larry; Larry would go to the Portland area to visit Mitch. As far as Phillip was concerned, he really didn't know him that well. It was only because Mitch had to pull out of the fishing trip that Phil and Larry wound up together.

Larry Wills, of Larry's Carpet and Furniture Cleaning, has never had a complaint against him with the Better Business Bureau, has never been delinquent in his house payments, has never had a tax lien, has never had any financial problems, and has never received any large sum of money that would significantly change his lifestyle. Larry Wills is an honest, hardworking man who enjoys hunting and fishing.

If Larry Wills is telling the truth about what happened the night of August 31, 1982, if Phil Champagne fell overboard exactly as John Robin said, then Phil Champagne is also telling the truth. The possibility makes Peter Richter almost as uncomfortable as when he took Mitch Champagne's deposition.

Mitch wept.

"Either Mitch Champagne is the greatest actor in the world, or he never knew that Phil wasn't dead," observed the astute Mr. Richter. "I find it hard to believe that in the ten years that Phil was gone, neither of his brothers ever helped him out. If one of them knew, it was probably John Robin."

Phil Champagne becomes irritated at the very suggestion of wrongdoing on the part of his brothers. "These insurance people are either stupid, crazy, or just plain greedy. They are going after John Robin for no other reason than he is one more person they can chase after, looking for a payoff. Hell, John Robin believed

I was dead and drowned years ago. He has had more than enough aggravation. They already want a default judgment against me for not being polite enough to let them know I wasn't dead, so why are they going after Mitch and John Robin?"

Seven hundred thousand dollars, Phil, $700,000.

"These characters see everything like it's some big conspiracy," continued Champagne, "and it amazes me. The Secret Service isn't much different. They thought I was some big international crime figure. Then again, they also thought I was that druggie, Ron Kollister."

Ah, yes, Ronald Edsel Kollister, alias Harold Richard Stegeman.

"We thought we were up against some sort of John Dillinger," said Lyle Workman with a hearty laugh, "and it turns out he is just a guy, this character, this sixty-two-year-old runaway from Oregon with a fake name and a real driver's license."

Kollister only attempted to use the Stegeman alias once. On June 7, 1985, he applied for a Florida driver's license in Martin County using Harold's name and date of birth. As Champagne already had a driver's license in that name, Kollister was busted for attempting to do what Phil had already done.

"Serves him right," Phil commented. "First come, first served."

Kollister failed to appear on the charge of using false identification in attempting to obtain a driver's license, and a fugitive charge was issued. The warrant is still outstanding.

"But the money," argued Richter, "how in the world did Phil Champagne wind up in Shelton as Harold Stegeman with all that money? Where did it come from, and how did he get it?"

The answer is Florida, and all because of those damn German marching songs.

"If you're a straight guy, if you aren't gay, Florida is a gold mine of wealthy women," observed Champagne. "What you have is a lot of women, many of them very well off, who have either lost their husbands or are recovering from failed marriages—sometimes several failed marriages. It's not about sex; it's about companionship and friendship. They want someone to talk to, go places with, and share their lives with. And the idea, if you're a man, is to give them your time, your attention, your affection, and never, ever, ask them for money. Let them throw it at you. Oh, you can let them know you could use it, let them know you have things you could do with it, but insist that you would never ask them for it. If they offer it, refuse it ... for a while. Then go ahead and take it."

Phil Champagne was not talking about stealing, or, if he is, he wouldn't admit it.

"Never, ever defraud them. Why would you want to do that? If you really have an idea of what to do with it, and you can make them a profit, do it. You're happy; they're happy."

Phil Champagne was one happy Floridian. The old saw of "a girl in every port" was an accurate appraisal of Champagne's lifestyle.

"I admit I probably did hurt some feelings. Maybe some of these women thought I was in love with them or thought they were in love with me. If I hurt them, I regret that. I don't want to live with hurting anybody."

Peter Donovan's trawler became a familiar sight up and down the Florida coast, waves of romance splashing in its wake.

"And they weren't all older matrons," Phil was quick to clarify. "Many of them were energetic youngsters with an appreciation of, shall we say, seasoned manhood."

Indeed, the dapper Mr. Donovan's luxury trawler,

replete with satellite television reception, full-sized refrigerator, microwave equipped kitchen, and all conceivable amenities, saw many a collegiate overnight visitor. Should the boyfriend of a Ft. Lauderdale lovely become suspicious of his bikini-clad paramour's Spring Break from their post-pubescent relationship, Phil would act paternalistically incredulous.

"Do you really believe a man my age would even know what to do with a young girl like that?" he would ask with an expansive gesture and widened eyes. "More often than not, they would buy it. Sometimes they would become a little jealous when they came back for more."

This was very different from the lifestyle in Gresham, Oregon, if what Phil had could by comparison be called a lifestyle. As Peter Donovan, Phil was a man on the move.

"Sometimes I would just go ahead and pay a month's moorage at a time, and more often than not, I would find a restaurant with a sea wall. I'd pull in, tie up, and after dinner I would tell them, 'Hey, I'm drinking and everything,' and they would say, 'Okay, just leave it there overnight.' It was no problem. I spent most of my time hopping from moorage to moorage, restaurant to restaurant, party to party, woman to woman. It was like I was on tour."

Having escaped his personal hellhole in Oregon, survived his watery demise in Washington, and reinvented himself as Peter Donovan, Phil Champagne was comfortable enough to dial the area code 503. Checking in with Alias Mike, he shared details of his miraculous transformation into a dancing, romancing playboy in the land of sunshine, nightlife, and generous matrons.

"You were right about Mexico, but I guess I had to learn the hard way. Besides, women are the best adventure."

"Those bastards aren't still after you, are they?" growled Mike. "Because if they are…"

Alias Mike was always eager to act out the more assertive aspects of traditional Western male behavior. Military tough and paranoid by design, he traveled America's highways "packin' heat"—a .45 automatic and a Remington shotgun, five in the tube, one in the chamber.

"Naw," laughed Phil, "that was long ago and far away. My life lately has been nothing but warm weather, cool breezes, and hot women."

In the course of the conversation with Mike, Champagne never inquired about his ex-wife, four children, elderly mother, or his two despondent brothers.

"If you can get away on some pretense, come on down and visit me."

Mike found a pretense.

Six weeks later, the two old pals relaxed aboard the trawler in Phil's Ft. Lauderdale moorage. The Florida moon, metaphorically extolled in numerous 1940 Avon mystery paperbacks as resembling a piece of luminous cheese, a dripping mass of silvery opalescence, or a cardboard cutout suspended mid-heaven by invisible wires, appeared to Phil and Mike as nothing more than a moon. They were entranced by a more immediate and less ethereal example of shimmering translucence—a vodka bottle. Good times, bad times, old times, and lifetimes of little consequence were the topic of conversation. Eventually, Phil asked the question Mike had anticipated. He asked it in a most offhand manner, his eyes averted as if by coincidence instead of design.

"What's going on back home?"

Best as he could, Mike brought him up to date. He related how John Legate was watching Seattle's local television news when the report of Phil's accident came on. John had called Joanne, who in turn called everyone else. Ed Grass heard it from his mother, who had heard it on the radio.

Phil poured himself another drink.

Mike explained about Joanne retaining Don Robertson to launch a suit against John Robin, Mitch's attempts to get Federal Kemper to settle on the Key Man insurance, and the dismal destiny of the ill-fated condominium project, which Phil had overseen before the San Juan sailing excursion. Mitch never realized a dime from what was known as "Cottonwood." Eagle Mortgage Company of Portland foreclosed, giving Mitch Champagne a guarantee that no subcontractor could sue him. Other than that, Mitch got nothing for his equity. As for realizing a profit, there was never one to realize.

"And," continued Mike, "there was a little matter of alleged insurance fraud."

Phil's grip tightened on the bottle. "Is someone going after Mitch?"

No, someone was going after Renee.

Peter Richter was long gone from Lake Oswego, Oregon, when Renee Champagne began her career as his hometown's premier cocktail waitress. Serving drinks by night and remodeling the former family home on Bel-Air Avenue by day, Renee invested innumerable hours and over $20,000 in improvements to both the interior and exterior of the Clackamas domicile, including new cabinets and floors.

One cold Oregon morning, about 3:00 a.m., Renee returned from work and built a fire in the fireplace before going to bed. A burning log later rolled from the hearth onto the carpet. There were no leaping flames, but there was plenty of smoke; Renee could have died from smoke inhalation. Fortunately, she awoke and survived.

Despite extensive smoke damage and understandable emotional upset, Renee felt assured that the danger had passed. She was wrong. The next day, while Renee was at work, the carpet, which had been secretly smoldering, flared to flames. The resulting blaze spread to the roof, engulfing the home, causing so much damage to the structure that the living room collapsed into the basement.

Thank God for insurance. Renee contacted family friend, real estate developer and occasional insurance agent, Ed Grass. It was Ed who had held title to the Champagne house and signed it over to Renee after her father's death. It was also Grass, unsuccessful at selling Mitch Champagne a Key Man insurance policy on Phil, who sold Renee a homeowner's policy with Foresters Indemnity. Ed helped Renee file her claim.

"She owned a valuable antique doll collection," recalled Grass, "and I had advised her that we couldn't get it insured without first having it appraised and getting a separate insurance rider. As fate would have it, the doll collection was out being appraised at the time of the fire. Foresters Indemnity accused her of setting the fire herself to collect the insurance after making sure her doll collection would be safe. Don Robertson, the same attorney who represented Joanne in her suit against John Robin, defended Renee."

Ed Grass testified on Renee's behalf, as did the daughter of famed true-crime author Ann Rule, a close friend and co-worker of Renee Champagne.

"Renee was devastated by that dreadful fire," confirmed Rule's daughter, "especially coming after the death of her dad. Being accused of insurance fraud was especially insulting considering how much hard work and effort she had put into that house."

"The jury found in Renee's favor," recounted Robertson. "She emerged vindicated and victorious."

"She was paid about $70,000," recalled Ed Grass, "and she deserved every cent."

Phil hadn't realized he had been holding his breath until the excess of carbon dioxide compelled him to exhale. Breathing again, he realized how upset he became at the thought of anything happening to his children.

"That's the hard part, Mike," confessed Phil. "I think about my kids every single day. I wonder where they are, what they're doing, what they're thinking."

"They think you're dead, pal. They think you're dead."

"Yeah. That was the idea, wasn't it?"

"Your idea," said Mike, but not harshly. "Your idea."

Phil leaned back and looked out on the Atlantic Ocean. Physical distance is not emotional detachment, and Champagne longed for the best of both shores—his Florida life and his Oregon offspring.

"I've never seen you look healthier or happier," remarked Mike, as if changing the subject or offering Phil another layer of justifications. He was doing neither.

"You can have the best of everything," Mike continued, "but you can't have it both ways."

There it was. Sitting in front of him, big as life, a living, breathing relic and reminder of who he had been and who, in truth, he would always be.

"Remember those damn bikers over in Eastern Oregon that time?" Phil said, changing the subject. He knew that Mike remembered those damn bikers. He also had no doubt that those damn bikers remembered Mike.

Phil and Alias Mike were out riding around in Mike's pickup. The two stopped at the Quick Spot convenience store for a fast lunch and a cold drink. When they emerged, seven ruffians on motorbikes decided to play the intimidation game. Off their bikes, the leather-clad bullies circled, taunted, and insulted the two men, grabbed their lunches, and tossed them to the pavement.

"Then they decided to screw with the pickup. I knew then Mike was gonna let 'em have it," recalled Phil. "When he reached in and pulled out his shotgun, they stopped in their tracks, but they didn't stop their insults. They backed off some, but they were still acting haughty because they believed he wouldn't kill them in cold blood."

Mike assured the boys he wasn't going to kill them; he was only going to shoot their horses. As the seven men watched in horror, Alias Mike pumped and fired round after round, even pausing to add a few fresh double-aught shells, until every motorcycle was unfit to ride and unsafe at any speed.

"There was gasoline running everywhere, the cycles were shot to hell, and these guys were begging him to stop. Even I was begging him to stop. Mike was always one hell of a shot," asserted Champagne. "When we were younger, we used to shoot silhouette targets. He could drill the eyes right out of 'em. When it came to firearms and accuracy, Mike was just about unbeatable."

The two shared several sun-baked days and balmy nights of nightlife and laughter, usually capped off with several rounds of German songs belted out in Dirty Nelly's, Shooters, or the Marina Inn and Yacht Harbor on S.E. 17th Street.

It could have been one of those nights, or it could have been another. It may have been a similar scene of inebriation inspired musical comedy anywhere along the Florida coast from Fort Pierce to Key Largo, from Shark Point to Siesta Key. Phil said it probably happened in Boca Raton, but it could have been Naples. It didn't matter where; it only mattered that it happened.

A man visiting Florida on business heard a familiar voice singing German songs in a cocktail lounge. A closer look revealed a face as familiar as the voice. The businessman, momentarily taken aback, continued monitoring the musical festivities for several minutes then slid unobtrusively to a pay phone. Had anyone overheard the conversation, the key statement made by the man on the lounge end of the line was simply this: "He is still alive."

NINE

I know personally several unusually creative photographers who have only a rudimentary understanding of photographic techniques…

—*Andreas Feiniger*
The Complete Photographer

O n the day of her arrest, Lyle Workman transported Barb Fraley from Ritzville to Spokane. They talked about how she was born and brought up on a farm in Wisconsin, and Lyle told her that she looked like a good old eastern girl.

"I apologized to Mr. Workman for refusing to give him my fingerprints, but I believed I was doing exactly what the lawyer said I should. He said, 'Don't say anything, don't do anything,' so I didn't. If my attorney tells me to do it, then there is no problem."

Lyle, ever the diplomatic investigator, did his best to assure Barb of confirmed legal representation.

"They'll get you an attorney; that's no problem. And I don't want you to talk to me. I don't want you to tell me anything."

Booked into the Spokane county jail, Barb relinquished her fingerprints. Harold and Rich paid for the impound on Rich's Subaru and drove home from Ritzville.

"I wanted to go back to the damn phone booth and

get the bad money that I hid there, but I was afraid it was a trap," acknowledged Harold. Back in Hayden Lake, Harold reached under his bed for a cardboard box. Inside were sheets of 100 to 150 counterfeit bills, which had not been cut out.

"With Rich's help, I burned everything I could think of burning, and still there sat the printing press. I believed that the law would be there any minute. I didn't want to be seen struggling to get the press into the van. After all, having a press isn't a crime."

Harold and Rich took all the plates, put gasoline on them, scrapped the images off with steel wool, cut them up into little slivers with scissors, and then put them in a box. Stegeman gave the inks, cleaners, developers, and unused plates to Rich, who hid them in the bushes under some old building boards. Harold scrubbed the ink spots off the floor and repainted the big table on which he had worked. He then hooked up his twenty-eight foot Nomad trailer to the van and drove up Highway 95 to Monte Lee's place at Cocolalla Lake.

"At that time, he lived in a rented trailer on the west side of the highway. I parked the trailer behind his. I told Monte I was in trouble, told him what I had done. He said he knew it anyways the minute I borrowed the hundred dollar bill." After moving the press out to Monte's, Harold stayed up at LeHew's place drinking vodka and fantasizing worst-case scenarios.

"I was worried about the counterfeit money hidden by the phone booth because I knew someone would find it, turn it over to the Secret Service, and they would immediately put two-and-two together. There was only one person in that phone booth with mud on his shoes, and that was me."

Harold Stegeman took another swig of vodka and surveyed his options while eyeing Rich, Monte, and Monte's son, Danny.

"Listen, fellas, I want some of you guys to drive me over there. I'm going to take a chance and try to get the stuff out of the phone booth. I think it's a trap, but what the hell. They're going to find it anyway if they haven't found it already."

It was 3:30 a.m. on the third day after Barb's arrest when Danny LeHew and Richard Fraley Jr. drove Harold to Ritzville in Richard's Subaru.

"Are you sure you can get away with this?" asked a nervous Richard Fraley Jr. as he slowed to a stop on the freeway.

"Remind me to tell you about my parachute jump in Georgia," Harold answered cryptically, slipping into the grass as the two young men drove away.

The sixty-two-year-old commando crawled flat on his stomach in the dead of a cold November night for about two hundred yards.

"I was about fifty feet from the phone, so I just lay there watching for several minutes. I saw nothing. I jumped up and darted to a spot just behind the phone booth. The money was still there. To me, that meant they were watching, that this was exactly what they were hoping I would do. Then again, maybe they had no idea the money was there, and it would be safe to pick it up. I crossed the freeway and put the bills by a post where I know I could easily find them again. Then I walked back down through the underpass to the next restaurant down from Perkins and met Danny and Rich. We drove back by the post, picked up the money, and went on back to Monte's place."

The vodka bottle was in Rich's car, and Harold began belting it back once they were on the road. By the time the three characters got back to Monte's, Harold was feeling no pain. He took out the money, now a soaking-wet mess, and spread the eighty bogus hundred dollar bills out on the bed to dry. Later, Harold moved part of them off, lay down on the bed, and went to sleep. When he woke up, several bills were missing.

Rich remembered the night of bottled vodka and bogus bills as one of rollicking frivolity.

"We were celebrating having recovered the money from the phone booth, and we were pretty drunk by the time Phil fell asleep. We were playing with the bills, grabbing handfuls of them. I took some, and Monte and Danny probably did, too, but I threw a good amount out the window of my car when I drove through Montana. I was hoping folks would find them and cash them, and that way it would throw the authorities off the trail. The only reason I did that was because I was trying to help my mom."

A hung-over Harold wrapped the bundled bills in plastic and then asked Monte LeHew Sr. to hide them somewhere safe. LeHew cleverly secured the bag under the doghouse.

The following day, Harold and Rich drove the van with the press to Budget Mini-Storage in Coeur d'Alene. He rented storage unit Number Thirteen, paid three months' rent in advance, and loaded the space with the press, ink, cleaners, and some unused plates. Stegeman paid cash and told the proprietors that he didn't have his driver's license with him and that he would bring the address later. He said his name was Larry Wills.

No longer trusting Monte LeHew Sr., Harold retrieved the plastic bag from under the doghouse and hid it in the woods temporarily. Later, he took it home to 1123 West Hayden and stashed it in a field.

"I was going to turn it in, but at the last minute I decided to keep it and see what would happen. Then I went back in the house and had more time to go through and destroy anything that I thought might be evidence. Somehow, I overlooked that negative they found in my briefcase. I don't remember how it got there. I must have had it with other scraps, numbers that I had cut out to paste in, and things like that. When I cleaned that stuff up and burned it, I simply missed that one little item."

There was another little item Harold missed—Barb. She was released from the Spokane jail on November 14. The only hitch was that Barb and Harold were not officially hitched.

"I don't want you living together," said the probation officer. "You're not married."

"Well, in Idaho, common law is that we are legally married," objected Barb.

"If you can get me a document and prove to me that you are legally married in Idaho, then that's fine. But otherwise, I'm sorry, Harold can't live with you."

Barb looked at Harold and Harold looked at Barb.

"This is where Harold lives," pleaded Barb. "We have lived together for six years. Am I supposed to throw him outside, or am I supposed to go out in the street?"

There was only one reasonable course of action, and Barb immediately suggested it.

"Yes," agreed Harold, "we might as well get married as soon as possible."

There was a significant time constraint involved because Barb was on electronic home monitoring which required her to wear an ankle bracelet that transmitted to a box sitting in the corner of the room. The box connected directly to her home telephone line, keeping authorities continually informed of her movements.

"When they put the monitor on, they give you what's called 'free time.' I had from ten in the morning until three in the afternoon to go as I pleased. It was mainly to seek employment."

They had an hour and a half before her free time was up, yet managed to make it all the way to the courthouse, get a marriage license, hotfoot it to church, and get married. Mr. and Mrs. Harold Stegeman made it home on time. Barb soon found employment as the manager of Spinardo's, a local Italian restaurant, and Harold was hired to do maintenance. Their employer, Glen Mooring, was informed of the charges against Barb. As she was innocent until proven guilty, he had no qualms about hiring a woman with such vast restaurant experience.

"I have worked in restaurants since I was thirteen," confirmed Barb to Tim Ohms during her trial.

"You've been handling money day in and day out since that time," added Ohms. "You must have substantially more experience than Mr. Bright; he's not that old of a person."

"I would imagine I have a lot more experience," Barb asserted, not seeing the intent of Ohms' questions. Perhaps he didn't blindside her, but the jury didn't miss his point: Why wouldn't a woman of her experience be even quicker to notice a counterfeit bill than Todd Bright?

"I have never seen any counterfeit money," insisted Barb. "I don't know about markings and all this stuff."

Indeed, Barb steadfastly maintained her wide-eyed innocence up to, through, and after her conviction. Between her arrest and trial were four months of Harold Stegeman waiting for the other shoe to fall.

"I kept expecting them to come for me any day. I kept telling Barb that they were coming for me because I was sure they were going to figure out that I wasn't really Harold Stegeman."

While Harold waited, Lyle worked.

"I had two distinct situations to deal with," Lyle said. "The first was helping Tim Ohms prepare the case against Barb; the second was trying to figure out exactly who this Stegeman character really was, and what, if anything, he was up to. We had Harold under surveillance soon after Barb was released and were amazed to find that he was going back into the counterfeiting business."

As it had been a few months since Barb got busted at the pancake house, Harold foolishly assumed he was no longer under investigation.

"I figured that they had not run a check on my fingerprints in the first place and had only kept them for their own records. After all, it wouldn't take that long to identify me if they had my prints. Hell, the FBI should be able to do that in a week or two at most."

The FBI had not been able to do that in three weeks, four, or even more. Workman was checking with Interpol as well, but he kept hitting dead ends.

"Maybe because I was broke, I decided to set the press back up and print some more counterfeit money just to have in case I needed it. Of course, I needed a place to do it because it wasn't something I could do around the house."

Harold found a shed on Government Way for only $180 per month. He rented it under the name of Frank Wincheski, a moniker already familiar to the folks at both Spokane's Inland Photo Supply and Litho Development and Research (LDR). According to customer service representative Marilyn Beck, the first time Wincheski did business with LDR was in August 1991. However, it wasn't until Special Agents Workman and Mikalson had shown her a photo of Stegeman that she recalled the incident.

"He said he was working on an invention, but he couldn't tell us what it was because he hadn't yet taken out a patent on it. But it had to do with printing plates. He didn't know what kind, size, or even what light source he would be using to burn the plates. He was very vague about the whole thing. I believe we gave him a package of six sample plates just to get rid of him."

At about 1:15 p.m. January 6, 1992, Marilyn Beck reported to the Secret Service that Harold Stegeman, alias Frank Wincheski, had just been in her store to purchase a light bulb. She recalled that he had also been in on January 2 to purchase a box of film. Beck noted the car's description and license plate number.

"It was an older, white Fiat station wagon, Idaho plates, #K87781."

A young white male waited in the car for Stegeman. Barb's kid; Barb's car.

"Barb's kid, Richard, could have got his mother off," remarked Lyle Workman, "if he had been willing to finger Harold and say it was Harold who was behind everything, but he chose not to."

Barb could have freed herself had she been willing to come clean with the Secret Service.

"At no time did I ever think that Barb would tell them anything," insisted Stegeman "I was right. She could have easily told them everything, especially with all the pressure she was under. They would have arrested me and let her go. Every time I think about that, I wonder how I could have been so lucky to have met her in the first place."

Harold Stegeman wanted nothing to do with American justice and knew less about its intricacies than he did those of offset printing.

"It took me quite a while to discover that I couldn't print without a printing press," admitted Stegeman, shaking his head in combined amusement and dismay. "I actually tried to make a counterfeit bill by printing directly off of the plate. As a matter of fact, I took an eight- to ten-inch piece of plastic sewer pipe…"

Harold stopped explaining and started laughing. "Well, it was obvious that it wouldn't work. I almost gave up on the entire idea until I found I could buy an old Multilith 1250 offset press for $350."

Not only were his printing efforts peculiar, his adventures in photography were ludicrously amusing.

"I realized I needed an actual size negative of a bill,

but a copy camera was out of the question because I couldn't afford one."

Harold drove to St. Vincent DePaul, a nearby thrift store, where he discovered a whole box of old cameras and purchased some Polaroid lenses.

"I made a box out of wafer board, about one foot square, drove an inch hole, and held the lens up to it to see if I could get any kind of an image that wasn't totally blurred. It seemed to work. I then screwed the lens on over the hole, caulked around it, and put lights on the other side of it and looked through. It was then that I realized I had to have something to case the image on. Well, I had read about how they used to use frosted glass in those old portrait cameras. I didn't have any frosted glass and didn't know where to buy it, so I just took a regular piece of glass and put strips of Scotch Magic Tape on it. It looked frosted to me, and it worked just fine."

The film Harold used called for f22 at fifteen seconds with 2,000 watts of light. He didn't know what f22 was, but he figured it didn't really matter. He was right.

Next, he needed a darkroom. Again, Harold used the wafer board and caulking, plus rubber weather stripping. "I built a box about four-feet by six-feet by four-feet right in the corner of the shed."

When Stegeman explained the Rube Goldberg design of his counterfeiting operation, the Secret Service agents were hard-pressed to keep from laughing.

"He had a Multilith 1250 but never used the machine to its capabilities," remarked Lyle Workman. "In his final printing process, he only printed one image per eight by eleven sheet of paper."

Harold had 500 sheets, and they cost him $18.

"Eighteen dollars, and I didn't have much money. Plus, I figured that 500 sheets with a hundred dollar bill on each one was a lot of loot."

He also had color trouble.

"I ended up, with my first batch, less than half of those 500 sheets printed on a yellow ivory-colored paper. It wasn't the right color, and it didn't feel right either. I tried different coloring processes, but I couldn't find any that really worked."

He attempted using watercolor, but it felt powdery when it dried. Next, Harold mixed yellow and black clothing dye with white watercolor powder.

"I kept mixing and re-mixing until I got a color that looked pretty good. I painted it on with a small brush and let it dry. I did both sides of the bill that way, then I made a cardboard pattern the same size as the bill and cut 'em out with an Exacto knife."

When all was said and done, he was not particularly pleased with the results.

"They looked real bad," admitted Harold. "The future batches were much better, but that first batch was real bad, plus I knew there was a flaw in them. But when I showed them to Barb, she said, 'My God, those look good to me.' That was October 15, and so we went on a little drive to Spokane to buy some strawberry-rhubarb pie."

Between the first October passes on Sprague Street and the ill-fated $18.73 November breakfast at Perkins Restaurant, Harold's counterfeiting enterprise went into a second printing.

"This time I went over to a paper supply outfit in Spokane and got some 100 percent, cotton fiber, twenty-pound bond that had a much better feel to it. I only changed the serial number. When I was done cutting, I had about seventy or eighty bills. I took the ones that were still on the full sheet and put them in a cardboard box under the bed. Then, a few days before we drove to Ritzville, I took Barb to downtown Coeur d'Alene and she cashed five or six of these new bills. One of them we cashed at an auto parts place, two of them were downtown in the new mall, one of them at the liquor store, and the others I don't remember. When a hardware store turned one of the bills down, I said that was enough because we were too close to home, and they still didn't look good enough to me."

They also didn't look good to the folks at the liquor store, the mall, or the auto parts store, and that is exactly why Secret Service Agent Workman was in Coeur d'Alene on November 6 when the call came in about the incident at Perkins.

"On the sixth of November we left in Rich's car for the Seattle area without really having an exact destination," recalled Stegeman. "We were just heading for an area that had a heavy business population in an attempt to cash some of the remaining bills, of which I had between sixty and seventy-five."

Barb had a different story. According to her, she was on her way to Olympia to visit her granddaughters.

"I never go out of town or anything without Harold. And my son was going because he wanted to see his kids, too."

"Yeah, that's right," agreed Rich. "We were just gonna go see my kids."

Instead, they saw Lyle Workman, and Lyle eventually noticed something peculiar about Barb's fingerprints. There was no print from the little finger of her right hand.

Tim Ohms immediately received an enthusiastic summons to Workman's upstairs office where Lyle thrust the prints under Ohms's nose.

"Tell me what ya see, Tim. C'mon, tell me what you don't see."

"Slow down, Lyle. You're losing me here."

"No pinky!" Lyle said as he slapped the prints. "No pinky, right? Now, does that HiCo video show a lady with no pinky? I would love to know."

Ohms and Workman checked the videotape. After being transferred to a still picture and subjected to substantial enhancement, the photo was consistent with someone missing the little finger from her right hand.

"Nobody has said that the person who gave them the counterfeit bill didn't have all their fingers," pointed out defense attorney Richard Sanger. "What they did in this case is determine that the defendant has part of a little finger missing, and then they went back and tried to bootstrap some sort of a non-identification with regard to a missing little finger out of an enhancement of a surveillance tape that doesn't show anything. I think it is highly prejudicial and doesn't have any relevance to the case."

Ohms pressed the argument, gaining the upper hand.

"The point is that it's consistent with the circumstantial evidence. In a circumstantial case, the government is entitled, under the law, to cast its net out there and bring in what's available."

The net also brought in Harold Stegeman. While the government prepared prosecution, Stegeman prepped his press on Government Way.

"Somewhere around the first of January, I went to the ministorage place where I had the press, disassembled it into three or four parts, so that I could move it by myself, and put it in the van along with other paraphernalia. I unloaded it all on Government Way, got some particle board, made a darkroom, made the camera, took the lens and the camera and drilled some holes, put my safe light in and a few odds and ends like that."

On January 10, Harold noticed a "long-haired kook" following him.

"It frightened me because I thought I was under surveillance by the Secret Service."

He was.

"Right then and there," Stegeman said, "I decided to

end the operation once and for all. I went back and took the darkroom down, sawed it up into strips of wood, put it in the van, took it home, and used it for firewood."

Stegeman sold his Multilith press to a hobbyist for $150, cut up plates, and put them in the trash at the Rathdrum, Idaho, garbage dump off Highway 53. He left a note for his landlord saying that he would be gone by the end of the month. Then Frank Wincheski left the keys hanging on a hook and walked away from counterfeiting forever.

"Barbara knew I had been up to something, but I didn't tell her exactly what and we didn't discuss it. She said, 'You're a damn fool.' I have to agree that she was right. No one else had any idea that I was up to it again. The only bills I had left were the ones I took from under Monte LeHew's doghouse. I put them in a raisin box on a shelf on the porch until I could decide what to do with them. Hell, I should have burned them right away because, after all, they weren't real."

According to Detective Inspector Brian Gibbs of the Royal Cayman Police Department, neither was Stegeman's Cayman Islands driver's license nor his residence permit.

"Both documents are bogus," declared Gibbs on May 11, 1992. "The driver's license number, 4135, has actually been assigned to someone other than Stegeman since 1975. Further, the address given for Stegeman on both documents, 182 Kings Drive, apartment 14, Georgetown, is not good. There is no such street as Kings Drive in Georgetown."

Detective Gibbs offered another enticing tidbit of information: The name Stegeman had been used for travel purposes by international criminals.

Interpol confirmed that Harold Richard Stegeman entered Costa Rica from Miami on January 12, 1985, using Costa Rica permit #399219, and returned to Miami the following day. While Interpol was unable to explain how the person using the Stegeman identification could make this international travel without use of a U.S. passport, they were able to report that former New Jersey Senate Minority Leader David Joel Friedland made an identical trip of one day's duration to Costa Rica from Miami.

Glib, charismatic, and touted as New Jersey's future governor, Friedland graduated from Rutgers University to enviable positions in both state politics and private legal practice. In the late 1970s, he was indicted and convicted for taking loan kickbacks. Friedland arranged for con artist Barry Marlin to receive a $4 million loan from the Teamsters, taking $360,000 for himself. The senator was also charged with jury tampering and tax evasion. Convicted in 1980, Friedland appealed his conviction and began cooperating with the FBI, helping them gain convictions against other corrupt officials. At the same time Friedland was helping the FBI catch the bad guys, he was preparing a $20 million double-edged rip-off of the Teamsters' Union.

The wily ex-senator arranged for the $20 million to be invested in Omni Funding, a mortgage company that he secretly controlled. The Teamsters believed Omni was lending on low-risk, FHA-approved projects at an interest rate of ten percent. In reality, Omni lent the $20 million to high-risk ventures piloted by entrepreneurs unable to acquire funding elsewhere. For the honor of Omni financing, the borrowers paid twenty percent instead of ten percent.

According to U.S. Department of Labor Special Agent Tom Sommero, Friedland also extracted kickbacks and partial ownerships in a variety of ventures, including a coalmine in Kentucky, a restaurant in Palm Beach, and bingo in the Dominican Republic.

As the ventures went belly-up, Friedland and his

criminal cohorts turned their ill-gotten personal profits of $4-6 million into South African Krugerands and Canadian Maple Leaf gold coins. Loaded with gold and anticipating indictments, Friedland devised a clever ruse. On Labor Day weekend 1985, shortly after the third anniversary of Phil Champagne's tragic boating accident off Lopez Island, David Joel Friedland faked his death in a scuba diving accident off the Bahamas. Again, the Coast Guard received a frantic call. Friedland was missing and presumed drowned

Unlike Phil champagne, Friedland didn't stay dead long. He resurfaced in London, granted press interviews, and contacted old cronies to shake them down for cash. Displeased with Friedland's tactics, his associates preferred to disclose his whereabouts to Special Agent Sommero rather than pay the former senator.

"We tracked Friedland through Kenya, Rome, and Hong Kong," confirmed Tom Sommero, "and finally to the primarily Moslem Maldive Islands off the West Coast of India. There are resort islands frequented by European and Japanese tourists and famed for scuba diving. As Friedland is an expert scuba diver, he loved it there. He also devised numerous schemes involving local investors, one of whom became suspicious and reported him to the authorities."

The reason for suspicion was the name on his passport—Richard Smith Harley—a name regretfully similar to that of a British mercenary remembered for arranging firearm shipments from Sri Lanka, which were used in a failed coup attempt. Intolerant of such behavior, island authorities detained Friedland for ten days, during which time they attempted to ascertain his identity. On the seventh day, they perused the latest Interpol Red Alert, recognized his face, and contacted the U.S. Department of Labor.

"On Christmas Day 1987, I arrived in Male on the

Maldive Islands," recalled Agent Sommero. "When Friedland walked into the room and saw me, he immediately turned to his captors, professed his belief in Islam, and begged for asylum. He insisted that his life had been threatened by Khadafi of Libya!"

No asylum was granted; no extradition agreement existed between the Maldive Islands and the United States. No matter. The unwelcome scuba diver was unceremoniously stuffed into Agent Sommero's departing plane. Imprisoned at the Fort Dix New Jersey Federal Correction Facility, David Joel Friedland no longer uses his home in North Miami Beach, his condo in the Bahamas, his lawyer in the Cayman Islands, or his false United States passport in the name of Harold Stegeman.

On October 31, 1985, sixty days after Friedland faked his death in the Bahamas, Harold Stegeman applied for a United States passport. This Stegeman was not David Joel Friedland. He was also not Ronald Edsel Killister. He was Phil Champagne.

TEN

Any new system is worth trying when your luck is bad.
--Heywood Brown

Don Robertson has sincere affection for at least one of the three Champagne brothers.

"Phil Champagne has always been a dear friend and valued client," remarked Robertson, "and in all the years I have known Phil, both before his tragic accident and after his reappearance, I have never known him to lie to me about anything."

Robertson was not as close to John Robin—it was Robertson who represented Joanne Champagne in the wrongful death claim against him—but their friction was not enough to ignite sparks of anger nor prompt one to speak too ill of the other.

"Robertson and I had somewhat of a falling-out back in about 1977," explained John Robin. "I tried to take him to court over a project he got me involved in. Strange as it may sound, in the end it worked out well for me. I wound up paying about three hundred thousand for some property, and sold it for six hundred forty thousand. Robertson may have been miffed that I wanted to take him to court, or perhaps," said John Robin with a laugh, "he was irritated that I came out of the deal making such a nice profit."

While Robertson endorsed the brothers' version of what happened over the long weekend in 1982, others suspected that the three brothers conspired to defraud Federal Kemper. Such cynics see conspiracy in every action, no matter how trivial.

"It seems a bit much," offered one of such persuasion, "that Phil, Larry, and John made such a spectacle of themselves at Boomer's Landing in Anacortes with the waitress and all that. Maybe they just did it to corroborate their story."

If such were the trio's intentions, they were ill-founded. Interviewed by insurance investigators on February 23, 1983, Boomer's Landing employees, Linda Carlsen and Priscilla Lemphuir, had no recollection of any group of three men being served on the night of the accident, nor did they recall waving good-bye to anyone from the window. The women emphasized that the restaurant was busy, and just because they couldn't recall the men or the incident didn't mean it didn't happen.

Conspiracy?

The concept of conspiracy implies that the participants are of like mind, share a common foundation, are united in their views and thoughts, and that their purposes are in harmony.

"John and Mitch didn't speak to each other for five years," noted mutual friend Ed Grass, "and all because they disagreed on how to do foundations."

John and Phil were close.

Phil and Mitch were close.

John and Mitch had nothing to do with each other.

"I was the first one to become a builder," said John Robin, "and then Mitch and Phil came into it, too. We worked together for a while, but that was years ago. Phil and I would set up jobs and scout property, and it was Mitch's position to supervise construction. He would make mistakes in pouring the foundation, and it ended up costing us twice as much as it should. I guess the thing that really made us break up the corporation was one particular incident, one particular foundation. The cost overruns for that foundation alone were about fifteen hundred dollars because Mitch and his foreman were pouring the walls thicker than they needed to be."

Displeased with the expensive foundation, Phil and John told Mitch how to set up the next job.

"It was ridiculous to throw the money away like that, so he agreed and said he understood," recalled John. "But I'll be damned if on the next job he'd gone and done exactly the same thing. When I confronted him about it, he said, 'Well, you build things the way you want. I build them the way I want.' I told him that the money he was spending was partly mine and that we had made a mutual decision as to how it should be done and it was his job to do it that way."

This conflict ended the Champagne brothers' triumvirate of cooperation. Mitch was about to marry his new wife, Dorothy, and she didn't think Mitch should take orders from his little brother. The assets of the corporation were divided. Mitch took five houses; Phil and John took the rest.

Mitch and John didn't speak, but Phil maintained positive relations with both. Not long before Phil's accident, John Robin took the initiative to patch things up.

"I went to where they were building and talked to him. I told him I thought it was ridiculous that we didn't speak to each other. After all, we're brothers. We might have some differences, but that is no reason to not even talk to each other. He agreed, so we shook hands and I felt better about it. We didn't ever become close, but at least we spoke once in a while."

Would John conspire with Phil to defraud Federal Kemper on Mitch's behalf?

"I didn't even know about Mitch having that insurance on Phil until Renee made allegations that I murdered her dad. She told the authorities that I was more an enemy than an uncle. I found this out from the state police when I had to go make a report about what happened. When I heard about the million-dollar policy, I thought, 'Oh, great. I lost a brother, his family is suing me, and now Mitch has got a million-dollar policy. The insurance people are going to be sure that brothers, in a situation like ours, they're gonna figure...'"

They figured. Perhaps Mitch and Phil conspired to defraud Federal Kemper, but left little brother John in the darkness of self-recrimination for the past ten years.

"There is no hard evidence that Mitch Champagne conspired to defraud the insurance company," reiterated Peter Richter. "No such charges have been, or will be, made."

Phil Champagne shook his head in amazement.

"See how crazy it gets? John and Mitch weren't that close, and if you knew Mitch you would know that he has never, ever, done anything wrong. He is the most law-abiding, conservative fellow on God's earth. I keep telling people that it was all my fault, all my choice, all my desire to get the hell out and start a new life. Even if I was near broke, it was better than what I was going through in Clackamas. Maybe if I had never left Florida, never come to Shelton, never made counterfeit bills, or maybe if Barb had used a real bill for that damn breakfast, no one would ever know that Phil Champagne was alive."

"I think he wanted his kids to know he was alive," remarked Barb. "It was tearing him up inside to not see his kids. I think a lot of what we went through was the result of Phil wanting his kids to find out that he was alive. He can't even think about them without getting all misty."

The mere mention of Kathy, Renee, Curtis, or Phil Jr. sends their father into wet-eyed reveries.

"When Ann gave me that beautiful trawler in Tampa, and I had it moored over by Waring's Marina, I wished the kids could see it, enjoy it, and spend time with me on it. But I knew that was impossible. Every time I did something new and adventurous, I wanted to tell them about it, share it with them, see the look in their eyes."

Phil began chuckling to keep from crying.

"If you ask the kids, they'll tell you I never liked to fly. In fact, it used to be a major trauma just trying to get me on an airplane. But when I was hanging out in Ft. Lauderdale, I even learned to skydive. I only jumped twice. Once at the airport with some folks I'd become friends with, and the other time in Georgia."

Formerly a man who never took chances, the resurrected Phil Champagne became fearless and daring.

"I figured since I had already died, what could possibly happen to me? When these new friends of mine in Ft. Lauderdale suggested I jump out of an airplane, I decided to go for it. I didn't much care for it, but it turned out to be a valuable experience in more ways than one. First, I learned I could do a simple static line jump. Second, I met a private pilot by the name of Stretch who was probably about as shady as I was, and more adventurous. We became occasional drinking buddies, and I had a standing invitation to drop by his place—a trailer near the airport—anytime I wanted. But then again, I always did have a knack for making friends."

Gregarious, outgoing, and courteous, Phil Champagne by any other name was still a man well met by those who'd meet him. A delightful conversationalist, he was forever expanding his circle of well-to-do friends and ne'er-do-well sea-going associates. Marinas, cocktail lounges, and Florida social occasions were all conduits of connections for the charming Mr. Peter Donovan.

"I used some other names too, or to be precise, I had identifications in other names. You might say I became mildly addicted to have several sets of false identification. If something went wrong, I could always be somebody else."

Something went wrong, terribly wrong.

"Would Mr. and Mrs. Champagne mind if we fictionalized this story?"

The question came from Patricia Brown, cohort and consort of television producer Anthony Spinner. They produced made-for-television movies, a genre with specific requirements.

"Television movies are female driven," explained Brown. "We are looking for women's stories, told from a woman's perspective, with a strong female lead."

Starring, for example, Elizabeth Montgomery or Valerie Bertinelli.

"Would they mind if we made Barb's brother a cop or a private eye? You see, we're thinking that maybe it would be interesting if it was Barb who unraveled the secret of Harold's true identity. She is innocent, of course. First, she has counterfeit bills, then a counterfeit husband. Now she must embark on a journey in which she searches for truth--the truth about the man she loves, and the truth about herself."

Really?

Phillip Krupp of Zev Braun Pictures, one of America's more successful high-profile producers of television programming and motion pictures, had no interest in fiction. He wanted facts.

"I have a moral obligation," explained Krupp, "to make sure this story is true before I attempt to sell it to my network. If I were going to fictionalize it, why bother buying the rights? I could make up my own story if I was interested in fiction. If this is true, I want it proven to me so that I feel comfortable with it."

Phil Champagne has no argument with either

approach.

"I don't care if they make me a cartoon mouse," said Phil. "And they can make Barb a leather-clad secret agent working undercover at a restaurant, brandishing a spatula in one hand and a .45 automatic in the other, if it makes them happy. But since this is a true story, and it is crazier than anything anybody could cook up, why don't they just tell it like it is? If they want proof, I'll give them proof. What proof do they want? Would they like Ann's exact address? The name of her lawyer? The only thing I will not reveal is the exact location of the dead bodies."

The dead bodies come before the Georgia parachute, and both come after Mike's first visit.

"Mike had actually flown to Florida in a private plane belonging to a relative of a former wife. He had cooked up some business reason why the guy couldn't come with me once they were in Ft. Lauderdale," explained Phil, "and Mike had to rejoin him later that night. Of course, once that ex-relative reads this book, he'll know exactly what was going on."

What was going on was vodka, conversation, and camaraderie. Mike and Phil arranged elaborate methods of renewed communication—letters to prearranged mail drops in different names, and cryptic messages culled from the pages of Moby Dick.

"It was kind of like a game or a puzzle. I would get a letter at the mail drop saying something like 'chapter five, paragraph two.' I would go to the library and look it up. Perhaps it was childish, but we both got a kick out of it."

Before Mike left, Phil shared the secret of trawler access.

"In case you come back sometime and I'm not around, here's how you get into the boat."

"Ah," observed Mike, "the famous Florida keys."

In mid-July 1985, Peter Donovan sailed southwest from Ft. Lauderdale past Key Biscayne, Key Largo, Plantation Key, Upper and Lower Matecumbe Keys, Long Key, Duck Key, and Boot Key by Marathon, and anchored slightly southwest of Spanish Harbor Key on the ledge of Looe Key National Marine Sanctuary.

"I took two couples out. I believe they were all county employees and I had met them at a local watering hole. There was Leonard Spain, John Bullard, Marie Nelsen, and Rosie somebody—I forget her last name. They were diving in forty feet or less, and I was doing my usual thing: sitting up on the blind bridge having a drink, looking toward shore."

Fewer than 500 yards west sat an Italian-made aluminum boat, close to 100 feet in length.

"It was an older model," recalled Champagne, "so he probably paid one million or one-and-a-half million dollars for it. A new model costs about six million dollars. You couldn't help but notice this one right off; it was bigger than most of the other boats anchored in the area."

Phil saw a human speck bobbing and waving far from the Italian craft.

"Jesus," thought Champagne, "that guy is too far away. Even if he dumps his tanks and tries swimming against a half a knot current, he's gonna be exhausted and not make it. It's way better than 300 yards."

Phil picked up his marine radio and tried contacting the ship. No response. He tried again. Nothing.

"Hey," shouted Phil to Leonard and John, "I'm going to go play hero and save this guy."

Grabbing the inflatable, eight-foot, U-shaped Zodiac, Champagne sped through the serene Atlantic and pulled out the man. Dazed, desperate, clutching, and thankful, the gasping and gulping gentleman explained that he had indeed run out of both air and energy.

"I didn't check his tanks to see if he was really out

of air or not. I just gave him a hand. He looked totally exhausted to me and seemed madder than hell that his own folks hadn't noticed that he was in trouble. He kept going on and on about how I saved his life. What happened to him was not unusual. I know because I scuba dive. You can go under and be quite surprised when you come up exactly how far away you really are.

Forty-five days later, David Joel Friedland would experience the same problem off the Bahamas.

Returned to his own ship, the recovering diver launched a tirade *en Español* against those who had failed to notice his predicament. "You must stay for a drink," insisted the rejuvenated victim, introducing Phil to a number of individuals whose names he would never recall.

"You saved my life; I am indebted to you forever. You're my brother. That is the Cuban way."

Phil knew nothing of "the Cuban way" but knew everything about accepting hospitality. He shared a drink with his new "brother," a fifty-year-old gentleman calling himself Raul Medina.

"He wanted to know all abut me, where I moored my boat—he even took pictures of it—and asked me all sorts of questions. I guess I stayed aboard about an hour. I tried calling over to my trawler, but nobody answered. This Medina character kept telling me that I was his friend for life, but I figured his enthusiasm would wear off soon enough."

It didn't.

Four days later, a long white limo pulled into Phil's Ft. Lauderdale moorage. Out stepped Raul Medina, with a woman of exceptional beauty and intrinsic allure.

"This is my sister," explained Raul.

Phil didn't care if she was his sister, his aunt, or a casual acquaintance. A dark-haired beauty with big dark eyes, five-feet, seven-inches, with "petite, unobtrusive breasts," Esperanza Medina attracted Phil's attention and activated his latent libidinous impulses.

"We have come to invite you to a party Friday night at my home in Boca Raton," exulted the gregarious Raul as Esperanza's eye contact proffered intimations of possible party favors.

Invitation accepted.

"There is a lot of money in Boca Raton, and much of it was invested in Medina's home. While not right on the water, it was close enough. It was a lovely place with attractive architecture and a well-manicured lawn. There must have been forty or fifty people there, and the party spread from the lawn into the house. There were folks shooting pool, and some car dealer who did a lot of television commercials was there. He damn near talked my ear off, but the party seemed perfectly normal. Raul was a charming host, introducing me to all these people. He seemed quite genuine, and Esperanza followed me around giving me that 'wait till I get my hands on you' look. All in all, it was a delightful affair."

The affair between Phil and Esperanza was launched two days later.

"She showed up alone at the moorage explaining that she wanted a better look at my boat," said Phil with a laugh. "I knew better than that."

Phil gave her the guided tour; she returned the favor. Two nights later, Esperanza decided she needed a change of clothes. She drove back to Raul's with Phil, where any objection to her overnight antics remained undisclosed.

"I became a semi-permanent fixture around the place," remembered Champagne. "I swam in Raul's pool, ate Raul's food, and made love to Raul's sister. The only problem was that he kept asking me what I did for a living, how long I had been retired, all that stuff. I forget the details of my impromptu recitation, but basically it was a reiteration of the 'retired builder from the Bay

Area' story."

One August afternoon, Raul took Phil into the den for a little heart-to-heart. Champagne feared it was about Esperanza, but instead it was about gratitude.

"I owe you my life," began Raul, "and I haven't forgotten it. It is only right that I do something to repay you, at least in part."

Phil's courteous attempts to alter Raul's tone were met with firm resistant and the offer of vodka.

"I have something in mind," continued Raul, pouring inebriation over ice, "something that could make you a good amount of money. But it isn't something I can discuss in detail. I will tell you this much: I want you to do something for me, and it is not something difficult. If you do this, I will give you $200,000."

Phil listened with renewed acuity.

"Before we discuss this further, I want you to come with me to my ranch up north, be my guest for a few days. You'll have everything you could want," Raul said, paused and added, "everything except Esperanza. Can you handle that, my friend?"

"*Ja wohol*," intoned Peter Donovan, stamping his foot.

"I love it when you do the German," exclaimed Medina, and he meant it.

ELEVEN

"All men should strive to learn before they die,
What they are running to, and from, and why."
                                    --James Thurber

Departing from Boca Raton's private airstrip the next day, the men flew far north, refueled mid-state, and transferred to a helicopter somewhere over the border.

"We followed the river, taking the curve, then we set down in a large open area surrounded by what I call 'scrub pine,'" remembered Champagne. "You wouldn't exactly call his place a ranch or a farm—it didn't have livestock—but it did have plenty of pine trees, bushes, and a well-built, recently remodeled split-level home.

"It was an older building, but well-preserved. I remember that the roof was Dutch gable and tile. But it was flat tile, not Mexican tile. It had a long, long driveway that went right into a big two-car garage. You couldn't go directly into the house; you had to open the door and go across the breezeway into the kitchen. It had a full basement with a rec room. No pool table, but a bar. It had kind of a restaurant look to it. There was a lot of dark wood and what I call European paneling—the kind with raised surfaces. It had French doors and windows with leaded, beveled glass. It was obvious money had been spent on the place."

The isolated location was not devoid of inhabitants. In addition to two hyperkinetic Dobermans, ten men awaited Raul's arrival.

"They all spoke Spanish, and a few of them spoke no English whatsoever. I was introduced to all of them, but I wasn't sure why. I just tagged along after Raul and he showered me with hospitality—food, drink, and a comfortable, relaxed atmosphere."

The atmosphere turned to isolation when Raul talked business with his Hispanic entourage. Phil, the obvious outsider, was placated with an unending supply of vodka.

"Raul still hadn't told me exactly what he was up to, or what it was he wanted me to do. The next thing I knew, I was left alone with the dogs and the caretaker."

Apologizing profusely, Raul explained that a sudden business matter required his attention. Phil was to stay at the ranch until his return.

"Now look," said Raul, "I'll be back as soon as I can. Draw your own conclusions, but I've got something I have to take care of, and I can't run you all the way back. You may be a bit lonely, but the caretaker will cook you anything you want, or you can cook it yourself. Consider this your own home," Raul offered graciously.

Phil didn't have his own home. He had his own boat, a floating habitat financed by a former flame, but "home" was an idealized illusion from his painful past.

Not wanting to offend his host or allow $200,000 to elude his grasp, Phil responded with polite assurances and self-deprecating humor.

"Go ahead and do what you gotta do. After all, if you wanted to kill me, I'd be dead by now."

Raul found the remark very amusing, gave Phil a manly hug, and took off with his entourage.

"I was left with those two dogs that were not too adept at conversation. It was monologue by me and tail wagging by them. Raul and the gang were gone a day or two, and a couple more guys showed up before he came back. They didn't speak English and were very surprised to find me there. I didn't know them; they didn't know me. We just nodded at each other and wondered what the hell was going on."

Cordoned off by lack of communication, Champagne ensconced himself on Raul's patio for relaxation and another round from the never-empty vodka bottle. From the kitchen's AM radio, immune from the shading effect of hills and trees, came on an old Elvis tune.

"To the King," intoned Phil to the surrounding scrub pine, "Who's been dead even longer than I."

Phil never had a thing for Elvis. The only connection between the peripatetic identity shifter Phil had become and the swivel-hipped icon of rock-'n'-roll was the 1072 Seattle World's Fair. Elvis utilized the Northwest locale for the cinematic musical *It Happened at the World's Fair*. Phil's oldest daughter, Kathy, became paralyzed while she was there over the summer vacation.

Accompanied by her maternal grandmother, Kathy took in the sights, sounds, tastes, and experiences of what was a singularly exciting event in the otherwise uneventful summer of '72. She rode to the top of the Space Needle, compared the speed of futuristic touch-tone telephones to the standard rotary dial models, eyed with suspicion the Communist Russians acting officious, and ate open-faced sandwiches advertised as "The Danish Delight."

Her back ached; her legs felt weak. Perhaps it was all the walking. The discomfort increased; her ability to control her legs decreased with alarming rapidity.

Assured by a local doctor that there was nothing wrong with her that a couple of aspirin couldn't cure, Kathy took the tablets and retired to bed. However, instead of gaining strength, she began losing control of her legs, and then lost all sensation.

Her father immediately took her to another physician who, at first, believed the young girl had polio. Phil knew that Kathy had been vaccinated and proved it to the doctor. Tests. More tests. Kathy's lower extremity sensations were soon limited to her big toe. After continued investigation, the culprit behind her creeping paralysis was found to be a spinal cyst growing between her should blades.

Surgery and physical therapy put the bounce back in her step. Within weeks, it was as if it never happened. Phil never forgot it.

Elvis's Golden Oldie segued into the Four Tops' "I Can't Help Myself"; Phil Champagne stood, stretched, and continued the interminable task of waiting for Raul.

"He returned jubilant, energetic, and radiating friendship. He was like a fresh summer breeze, warm and buddy-buddy-like as ever. Raul appeared as pleased to find me as I was to see him return. To tell the truth, I was bored to tears."

There were only two ways out of Raul's country estate: helicopter or highway. Phil was a welcome guest, but five land-locked days of canine conversations and hand signals with strangers was not Champagne's idea of a rustic vacation. He kept reminding himself of why he had been invited. Money. Lots of money. Phil found that the contemplation of significant amounts of money was an excellent antidote to boredom.

Finally, Raul ushered Phil into his dark-paneled study. Sitting behind his large desk, Raul scratched his chin and seemed to be in doubt as to where he should begin. He swiveled his chair around and pressed on a panel, which popped open revealing a brown banker's box. Raul retrieved it, placing it on the desk.

"It wasn't a secret panel, nothing mysterious about it, and the box was as plain as can be. But the cash—now that was impressive."

Raul smiled as Phil eyeballed the fresh bills.

"Two hundred thousand dollars, my friend, and I promise you that it is all yours for doing what will be a very simple and enjoyable task."

Champagne attempted to appear relaxed and confident, but the two preceding days of infinite boredom had him leaping inside like a pup welcoming his master.

"You do a remarkable German accent, Peter," began Raul, leaning back in his chair, "and that makes you perfect for what I have in mind. You see, there is a boat sitting in the Cayman Islands. German registry. It is a simple matter. The German owner must appear with the appropriate papers to have the boat released. Simple. I will provide you with everything you need— the papers, a crew, as they say, 'the works.' All you do is be a convincing German. Show up, sign the papers, and have a pleasant boat ride back from Grand Cayman to Tampa. We will be waiting for you, bring you back, and this money is yours. Well?"

It sounded simple. Not too simple, but simple enough. Something was obviously off-kilter about the enterprise, but Phil Champagne knew he was not being paid $200,000 to ask questions.

"They won't release the boat to a Cuban," added Raul, referring to himself, "or to a Mexican or to a Panamanian. German ownership is what the papers say, so a German it must be."

Phil nodded as if it all made sense. Perhaps it did; perhaps it didn't. The money, however, made perfect sense, and in his mind, Champagne was already spending it.

"Any German in particular?" asked Champagne in an offhand manner. Damned if he was going to appear to be an ingrate.

"Yes, your name is Klaus Kruger. That is the name on the papers."

"What about identification?" Phil asked, as if forged papers were something unique and wondrous.

"Identification that appears to be authentic is not difficult to produce. We'll take some pictures and, well, it is a small matter with which you need not be concerned

"I understand," said Champagne, and he certainly did.

Raul smiled and picked up a pen. Ripping a slip of paper from his desktop note pad, he spoke as he wrote.

"This money is for my gringo friend, Peter Donovan, to whom I owe my life."

The note went into the box, the box went into the wall, and within the week, Phil and Raul went to the Cayman Islands.

"A few days before we took off, we went to Raul's house and took some pictures—passport photos—and I did some signatures. It wasn't long before they had an authentic-looking German passport and some other vessel document in German, which I couldn't read. We left from the Miami airport, and I was sober. I know that because I still am not crazy about flying if I'm sober, so I wasn't in a very good mood."

Adding to Phil's discomfort, his travel companions conversed in Spanish for the flight's duration.

"There were about six of us that went to Grand Cayman," recounted Champagne. "Raul, the guy that he was always with, who I don't believe spoke any English, and these other guys who I didn't know. No women. I don't know what the hell they were talking about. Every once in a while Raul would apologize to me for not keeping up a conversation I could follow. Under the circumstances, it all seemed normal."

Landing in Grand Cayman, Phil was transported to a hotel where he was introduced to the Norwegian captain who would bring the boat back to Florida.

"Then we all just screwed around, had dinner, and

didn't discuss anything much at all. The next day some fellow Raul knew on the island, a lawyer or something, took us down to the docks. Everyone was laid back, relaxed, but businesslike. I didn't have to go in and demand my boat, or really do much of anything. It didn't bother me a bit to do this; I wasn't nervous at all. I had my part down to perfection."

Klaus Kruger said his lines, waved his papers, signed a book, and identified the Norwegian as the captain of his ship.

There was the small matter of a fine, but another glance showed that it had been paid in full. No problems. No problems at all.

Raul didn't accompany Phil aboard the ship, but planned to fly back to Ft. Lauderdale.

"You guys get on your way," advised Raul. "I'll arrange transportation for you from Tampa and meet you at the house."

Phil, the Norwegian, and four others piled into a small boat on the docks, fired it up, and headed on out to get the ship underway. They traveled without incident around the western tip of Cuba and headed for Florida.

"The vessel was originally built as a whaler. It was 100 feet, steel, with Mercedes diesel engines. It was a beauty."

Phil Champagne, alias Peter Donovan and Klaus Kruger, was a happy man.

"This is the easiest money I have ever made in my life," thought Phil. "I'll do this act as many times as they want."

Slicing through the open water, Phil Champagne felt oddly free. Perhaps it was the exhilaration of having performed so perfectly; perhaps it was anticipating of the $200,000. It may also have been the personal pride of knowing he had pleased his pal Raul.

Phil watched the ship's captain pour himself another

cup of thick, black coffee.

"We have a saying in Norway," the captain said with the dourest of expressions. "It doesn't take a lot of water to make a good cup of coffee."

It looked more like wet tar than fresh java.

"Bet you can eat that stuff with a spoon," commented Phil, still doing his German. The captain didn't laugh; he only nodded. "Raul must have really wanted this boat," continued Champagne, dispensing with the Germanic intonations, "and I can't blame him. It's a beauty, isn't it?"

The captain laughed and took a noisy slurp from his steaming mug.

"You better believe it. What's even more beautiful is the money he's getting for what's in the hull."

Phil forced a smile.

"Yeah? What's in the hull?"

The stocky Norwegian raised his eyebrows, and Champagne suddenly had memories of himself desperately searching for markers in Lake Okeechobee.

"If you really don't know," remarked the captain as if Champagne knew everything, "all I can say is, 'Welcome to Crime on the High Seas.'"

TWELVE

Truth is not a matter of opinion. Truth may be investigated and ascertained.

--Buddha

On March 4, 1992, U.S. State Department Diplomatic Security Division Special Agent Bob Kircher reported to Lyle Workman that a person using the identity of Harold Stegeman had made application for and received a U.S. passport on October 31, 1985, in Tampa, Florida.

On March 5, 1992, State Department Special Agent Mike Hudspeth obtained certified copies of both a birth certificate and death certificate in the name of Harold Richard Stegeman. Hudspeth confirmed that the real Harold Stegeman died November 4, 1945, in Dade County, Florida at the age of eight. Hudspeth immediately faxed this information to Lyle Workman at the Spokane office.

On March 6, 1992, three days before Barb's trial was to begin, an arrest warrant was prepared for Harold Richard Stegeman, a.k.a. John Doe, for one count of conspiracy to pass U.S. Obligations.

"Barb and I were working at Spinardo's Italian Restaurant, getting the place ready to open. There were painters and carpet layers waiting for us when we got there," related Harold. "We pulled up in our van ready to go in, unlock, and do the usual stuff. Suddenly, Workman's buddy [Special Agent Mikalson] whipped in driving a Blazer, and pulled around as if he was trying to block me. I couldn't figure out what this long-haired, goofy-looking guy was up to. He jumped out, pointed a gun across the hood of his Blazer and started yelling, 'Get up against the wall! Don't move. I'll shoot.'"

Mikalson did not arrive alone. Perhaps fearing that an unarmed sixty-two-year-old man and a diminutive waitress might try to intimidate him, several four-wheeled law enforcement vehicles pulled up to lend needed emotional support.

"Don't you dare pull a weapon!" Harold was warned.

"Check her purse. She might have a gun in there!"

If Harold Stegeman had not been on the receiving end of such noisy indignities, he may have found them amusing.

"First, the deputy sheriff has me up against the wall, then I get the handcuffs, and then I gotta get in the sheriff's car. The deputy asks me if I have any weapons on me or anything that I could use to hurt him."

Harold closed his eyes, shook his head, and laughed the soft laugh of experience and forgiveness.

"He's got an old man handcuffed, and I'm supposed to pull a weapon on him?"

While Harold was cuffed, Barb was confused.

"They didn't tell her anything; they didn't even tell me why I was being arrested. It was all guns and screaming and barking orders. My God, what a bunch of Boy Scouts. I only had time to tell Barb one thing—I told her to get rid of the bills in the raisin box on the front porch."

Unflappable as ever, the cooperative Mr. Stegeman assured his captor at he posed no threat to their safety.

Barb's pleading eyes searched for Harold in the back of the deputy's car. He gave her a smile and a memorable parting comment.

"It makes me lose all respect for law enforcement officers when they act like this."

Lyle Workman awaited Harold's arrival at the Kootenai County Jail. He didn't know who Harold was, but he knew who Harold wasn't.

"We Mirandized him and he verbally waived his right to an attorney at that time," recalled Workman. "During preparation of a Personal History Summary, he provided information still using the name Harold Richard Stegeman."

Harold confirmed that he had resided in Hayden Lake, Idaho, with Barb and two of her children, Jerry Fraley, age sixteen, and Leanna Fraley, age thirteen, since 1990. Harold was honest when he told them he lived in Florida from 1984 until 1986, although he falsely placed his residence in St. Petersburg.

"From 1949 until 1984 Stegeman said he resided in the Cayman Islands with a man he believed to be his uncle, but 'wasn't sure whether he was an uncle or not,' Frank Lattimer," said Lyle Workman. "When we asked him why he did not ask questions about his parents and why he was placed with this friend/uncle, he indicated, 'I never asked Frank Lattimer about my family. He wasn't the kind of guy who talked much.' From 1937 until 1949 he supposedly resided in Miami, Florida, with Lattimer, who he claimed was deceased."

When Harold was done reciting the fabricated history of his life, Workman let him know the jig was up.

"We know you're not Harold Stegeman. The real Harold Stegeman died at the age of eight. The U.S. State Department is preparing a warrant for the use of this false identification in preparation for an application for the passport you received in October of '85."

If Workman expected Harold to become unnerved in the face of this shattering revelation, his expectations were in vain.

"He made it clear that he was not the least bit concerned about such charges as false identification, driver's license, and such because they would only result in minor fines or insignificant sentences. He did speak of wanting to help his wife, whose trial was about to start, but thought it would be best to contact an attorney for what he termed 'advice on other issues and events in his life.' As always, Harold, or whoever he was, was a true gentleman."

Now that Workman and Stegeman both knew Stegeman wasn't Stegeman, the obvious question was: "Who is he? Really?"

"I'd love to tell you everything, fellas. I really would," said the affable Mr. Stegeman, "but if I do, it won't be because of involvement with the Secret Service."

Workman and Mikalson were more baffled than ever.

"For all we knew, we were dealing with an international criminal, possibly the mastermind of any manner of nefarious undertakings."

The United States of America vs. Barbara Ellen Fraley went before the Honorable Fred L. Van Sickle on Monday, March 9, 1992. Timothy Ohms represented the United States of America, and Richard Sanger represented Barb, Harold Stegeman's new bride.

"This is a criminal case," explained Judge Van Sickle to the jury, reviewing some of the basic rules. "First, the defendant is presumed innocent until proven guilty. The indictment brought by the government against the defendant is only an accusation and it is nothing more. It is not proof of guilt or anything else. The defendant, therefore, starts with a clean slate."

The arrest of Harold Stegeman also wiped clean a significant portion of defense attorney Sanger's approach to the case.

"Do you really think it was a coincidence that they

arrested Harold immediately before the trial was to begin?" asked an understandably cynical Sanger. "Or was it a coincidence that the government did a highly publicized search of the Stegeman home on the last day of the trial, the same day Barb testified on her own behalf, and the day before the jury went into deliberations?"

Sanger did not find the supposedly innocent synchronicity any more amusing than he did the photomontage of possible suspects shown to witnesses at the trial.

"All of the witnesses said the person who passed the counterfeit bill in their particular business had short hair. The government investigators picked up on that and put together a photo montage in which they placed only one person with short hair: Barb."

When Lyle Workman took the stand, Sanger hammered him about the montage.

"Is it an accident, Agent Workman, that in the montage Barbara Fraley's picture is larger than the pictures of the other ladies in the montage?"

"Yes, it is. I cannot explain that," answered Workman.

"And is it an accident, Agent Workman, that Barbara Fraley's picture appears in the center of the montage?"

"Entirely."

Sanger portrayed Barb as the sandbagged fall guy for a government unwilling to pursue the true culprits who were still passing bills long after Barb was arrested.

"They figured they had who they wanted, so they didn't look any further," Sanger said. "And, it is important to note, they didn't look any further in any of the other fifty-one cases to determine who passed those particular bills. To put this in further perspective, long after Fraley's arrest, a number of these bills, some fifty of them, appeared in northern Idaho, eastern Washington and even western Montana. Barb wasn't passing those; we know that for a fact. She was under strict home monitoring and was certainly not running around three different states cashing counterfeit bills. But on November 6, they actually apprehended her after having passed a counterfeit hundred-dollar bill at Perkins in Ritzville. That does not mean that she knew it was counterfeit."

Sanger was quick to apprise the jury of the judge's forthcoming instructions.

"You will be instructed by the court that the mere passing of a counterfeit bill does not a guilty person make."

Barb would have you note that Richard Yokum stole the purse from the bowling alley and that Harold Stegeman gifted her innocent self the phony hundreds.

Timothy Ohms, armed with impressive visual aids and a casting call of prosecution witnesses, may have outgunned Sanger in the courtroom even without arresting Barb's best defender. Harold was to take the stand and spin a believable yarn in Barb's behalf, explaining how she came into possession of several hundred-dollar bills of dubious authenticity.

The story, later related to a disbelieving jury by an ill-prepared Barb, was that Harold sold a trailer for cash, the purchaser never came for the trailer, they couldn't remember his name, and the money turned out to be fake. She would have been better off sticking to the original "cashed the paycheck at the supermarket and this is what I got" story.

Tim Ohms trotted out significant participants to describe the damaging particulars. Todd Bright, manager of Perkins, took the stand with confidence and well-deserved self-assurance.

"As soon as I was given the bill, I knew it was fake. It was extremely coarse. It felt like a brown paper bag. At first, I thought it was a joke. I thought, 'No, you're kidding me.' It was that obvious. It had no red threads in it, and there were blotches of ink on the borderline of the bill."

Ohms attempted to cast Barb's behavior at Perkins in the most incriminating light, implying guilt because she had "attempted to flee." Sanger condemned the inference as unwarranted and irresponsible.

"Her son, Richard, was the driver and owner of the only vehicle they had," pointed out Sanger, "except when they were standing in front of the cash register, Richard stayed right next to the Perkins Restaurant outside the front door with the manager during the entire process. The only one who didn't stick around was Harold Stegeman."

If found guilty, Barb faced the possibility of seventy-five years in jail—fifteen years maximum on each of five different counts of knowingly passing a counterfeit bill.

"Her best bet—her only bet—was to make sure all the blame fell on the man who called himself Harold Stegeman. Sanger told the jury about Harold's arrest, the card from Inland Photo Supply with the flipside list of counterfeiting ingredients, Stegeman's alias of Frank Wincheski, Barb having "learned only Friday that he's not Mr. Stegeman," the government not knowing who he was or where he was from or "even if he is a citizen of the United States."

Wednesday afternoon, following Workman's testimony confirming the counterfeit nature of Stegeman's identity, Richard Sanger explained to Judge Van Sickle his desire to put the recently arrested Harold on the stand.

"Your Honor," began Sanger, "I'll be very honest with you about this because I don't want to get in any trouble, but I want the jury to see Mr. Stegeman and get some idea of what kind of person he is."

Harold and his court-appointed counsel were in another courtroom in the same building for a pre-release detention hearing. Harold could be tracked down and in the witness box within thirty minutes.

"I'm not putting him on the stand expecting him to testify at length and answer all of my questions," Sanger continued. "I fully expect to ask him questions such as, 'You manufactured this money, didn't you?' and 'Who are you?' and, 'You gave your wife some of this manufactured money without telling her, didn't you?' And I expect him to take the Fifth Amendment. And I am expecting him to be advised by the court in front of the jury of his Fifth Amendment rights. Now, if that is improper or if the court disapproves of it, that's fine."

It wasn't until 3:30 p.m. and out of the presence of the jury, that Van Sickle gave his opinion. In his review of the law, he determined that Mr. Stegeman may not be unavailable for inquiry by either side.

"I would give what's called the neutralizing instruction to members of the jury," explained the judge. "The court has determined that while there have been references made in this trial to Mr. Stegeman, the jury may not draw inferences from that fact or from the fact that Mr. Stegeman did not appear as a witness in the case."

Van Sickle did allow Sanger to make inquiry of Harold outside the presence of the jury. Harold R. Stegeman, the man who once elevated Shelton's Barbara Fraley to the ranks of well-kept women and pampered lovers, the former Mr. Moneybags who treated her as if she were plated in gold, was asked to take the stand.

"Please come forward here, sir. Please raise your right hand."

Whereupon, Harold R. Stegeman, having been first duly sworn in at 3:35 p.m., testified.

THIRTEEN

You know what charm is: a way of getting the answer yet without having asked any clear questions.
                                                    —Albert Camus

I t was as if every atom in the universe ceased to move. The attention of every human mind and heart within the confines of the courtroom focused on the charming gentleman who swore to tell the truth, the whole truth, and nothing but the truth.

"I had no idea what he was going to say," recalled Tim Ohms. "He was doing to have to say one of three things. He was going to say his name was Harold Stegeman, which was false; he was going to have to reveal his true identity; or he was just going to keep his mouth shut. I tried to be prepared for whatever it was he had to say. He only had so many options."

Barb sat transfixed. This was it. She was about to find out exactly what was going on with Harold. Since the moment of his sudden arrest at Spinardo's, she hadn't received a comprehensible answer from anyone. She had no idea why Harold was taken away; even Harold hadn't been told her why he was picked up until he was in the county jail.

"After Harold was arrested, I kept calling around trying to find out what they did with him and where they took him. I finally found out that he was taken from the jail to the federal building because he had to waive something, whatever that means. When I got into the elevator of the courthouse, there was Lyle Workman. I immediately asked him why Harold was picked up."

Lyle erroneously, but understandably, assumed Barb knew everything about the man to whom she was married and replied, "We received Harold Stegeman's death certificate."

Barb didn't get it. Now with her handsome husband under oath, perhaps she would understand.

The court clerk spoke: "Would you state your full name and spell your last name for the court and record."

"Your Honor, my attorney instructed me to inform the court that I would like to invoke my right under the Fifth Amendment to remain silent. With all due respect, sir."

"I understand, sir," responded the judge.

Barb did not understand at all.

Sanger began direct examination.

"Mr. Stegeman, what is your true identity?"

"I respectfully refuse to answer that question."

Harold saw the color drain from Barb's face.

"Did you manufacture counterfeit money and give some of it to your wife?"

"I refuse to answer on the same grounds."

Barb felt faint.

"Are you going to answer any of my questions, or do you refuse all questions on the same grounds?"

"I refuse to answer on the same grounds."

"You may step down, sir."

Richard Sanger approached the bench; Barb approached delirium.

"I have subpoenaed Mr. Stegeman and tried to get his testimony. At this point, Mr. Stegeman was not available to help the defense. Maybe at some later point he would be."

Ohms, knowing Sanger would want the judge to grant a continuance, allowing time to obtain additional evidence helpful to Barb, was not shy in voicing his objections.

"Your Honor, this defendant is charged with passing counterfeit currency. The government has not made any allegations as to who manufactured it. There's substantial evidence, to not only with regard to the passing of money at Perkins, but with regard to four passes of counterfeit currency occurring on one day, from which the jury could infer guilty knowledge on the part of the defendant. I don't see how the testimony of an individual saying, 'I gave this money of someone,' would be relevant for purposes of determining guilty knowledge at that point in time. I allowed Mr. Sanger to delve as deeply as he wished into any information concerning Mr. Stegeman, and I feel that he's had ample opportunity to raise any inference he wishes about Mr. Stegeman's character or his involvement in criminal conduct."

The difficulty was in determining when and if Harold Stegeman would be available to testify for the defense. It would be never. Van Sickle did not grant a continuance, and Sanger didn't expect him to. The only witness left for the defense was the defendant herself.

Sanger took a good look at his client. She did not look good. She appeared devastated and disoriented.

"My client is extremely tired at this point in time after three days in trial," pleaded Sanger, "and she did not sleep very well last night. I beg the court's indulgence in allowing us to recess for the day and begin with her testimony first thing in the morning."

The jury was brought back into the courtroom at 3:45 p.m.; court adjourned at 3:48 p.m.

On March 12, 1992, the proceedings of the final day of Barb Fraley's trial began at exactly 9 a.m., with defense counsel Richard Sanger making a motion to dismiss count one of the five counts against Barb—the incident at HiCo Exxon.

"There is no evidence in the State's case from which a reasonable person could find the defendant guilty beyond a reasonable doubt," insisted Sanger, taking issue with the videotaped evidence. "The government conceded in its opening statement that the jury could not make an identification from the videotape.

"They also said the tape did not show the little finger of the suspect's right hand. The suspect was either missing a finger, or the camera couldn't see it. Barb has a little finger on her right hand; only the very tip of it is missing.

"Agent Workman stated that the clothing worn by Barbara Fraley in Ritzville is the same as the clothing seen in the HiCo incident. However, these witnesses admit that they cannot point to any distinguishing features of the clothing, that they were judging from a black-and-white photo, and that they could not tell the color of the clothing in the photo."

Sanger then raised an unintentionally amusing issue.

"Everybody knows that they have videotape cameras in the HiCo stores right out in plain sight for God and everybody to see. Any knowing counterfeit passer wouldn't be worthy of his trade to go in front of a camera with a counterfeit hundred dollar bill."

No one claimed Barb was worthy of the trade.

Judge Van Sickle denied Sanger's motion, and at 9:30 a.m. Barbara Le Hew Yokum Fraley Stegeman took the stand on her own behalf. While she was being placed under oath, U.S. Magistrate Stephen Ayers of Coeur d'Alene, Idaho, signed a search warrant for Harold Stegeman's residence and the adjoining trailer.

"The purpose of the search," explained Lyle Workman, "was to find the passport he obtained using false identification. That's all they were looking for."

The search began at 11:50 a.m., exactly twenty minutes before court took noon recess. Special Agents Mikalson, Rosdahl, and Kircher, accompanied by Kootenai County Deputies Brodeur and Street, encountered no opposition from the home's only occupants, thirteen-year-old Leanna and sixteen-year-old Jerry.

The passport (real), Cayman Island Resident Permit #3408 (fraudulent), Social Security card #594-36-7447 (valid), and Dade County Birth Registration card #43288 (authentic) were all found in the master bedroom closet.

There was more.

From the same bedroom, Special Agent Rosdahl retrieved a brown vinyl briefcase containing Barb Fraley's 1987 and 1988 tax returns. It also contained two photographic impressions of a Federal Reserve Note. One photo was a Bank Seal. The other was the lettering "This note is legal tender for all debts public and private."

"Whose briefcase is this?" Agent Rosdahl posted the question to sixteen-year-old Jerry Fraley. Jerry said it belonged to Harold Stegeman. In fact, he was sure of it. Rosdahl then placed a call to Special Agent Neil Goodman of the Spokane field office, who obtained authorization from Magistrate Ayers for an additional search warrant to look for materials and equipment used to manufacture counterfeit Federal Reserve Notes.

"What's occurred here that is very unusual," commented Timothy Ohms several months later, "is that you have an investigation of someone who could potentially be a significant witness for the defense occurring while the defense is in a jury trial. You don't usually have a situation where the trial is Monday, and Thursday you are out searching another suspect's house, which also happens to be the defendant's house, and you find evidence. In this case, the proverbial smoking gun— the photographic impression of a Federal Reserve Bank Seal."

It was exactly 9:30 a.m. when the court clerk asked Barb to state her full name and spell her last name for the court and jury.

"Barbara Ellen Fraley. F-R-A-L-E-Y is what my name was at the time. My name now is Barbara Stegeman. S-T-E-G-E-M-A-N. I believe."

Barb had no way of knowing her own last name and slim chance of overcoming the ignominious implications of the prosecution's well-executed multimedia presentation. Ohms had trotted out employees from Perkins, Señor Froggy's, and every convenience store and pie purveyor with whom Barb had supposedly come in contact. The jury was treated to videotapes, photo enlargements, and in-depth explanations of intaglio printing worthy of PBS. The twelve-person panel of her peers even heard testimony from Sharon Burgerson, the attractive nurse's aide from Holy Family Hospital who bought a twelve-pack of beer, five lottery tickets, and three bags of M&Ms at HiCo Exxon.

Barb told her story to the jury answering questions from Ohms and Sanger. She recounted the woes visited upon her by providence, matrimony, and entrepreneur restaurateur Harold Stegeman. Barb denied any knowledge of counterfeiting in general and passing bills in specific, insisted she couldn't find the HiCo Exxon even when she went looking for it, and related the tale of Harold giving her $1,000 in one hundred dollar bills after selling a trailer.

"He says the guy gave him money down on it, but the guy never came back," explained Barb, "but the trailer is still sitting there waiting. If the guy ever comes back, the trailer is his."

"Is it common," asked Ohms of Barbara, "for Mr. Stegeman to give you money in hundred-dollar denominations?"

She confirmed that Harold had often given her

money—plenty of money.

Did Barb, before Harold's arrest, have any reason to believe that her husband was involved in criminal activity?

Barb wept.

"Nothing would surprise me now after finding out that he's not the person I married. He could be involved in murder as far as I know. I don't know what he's been involved in. He's not the person he said he was."

"But he always had money, didn't he?"

"Yes, that's correct."

"Did you ever have any idea how much it was?"

"No, but I know he put a lot of money into the restaurant."

"Did you ever meet any of his friends?"

"No. He never had any friends. He was a loner type of person."

At 12:10 p.m., when Tim Ohms and Richard Sanger had exhausted all avenues of direct and cross-examination, the defense rested. During the lunch break, Ohms heard news from the Secret Service, which he felt compelled to share with Sanger and the court.

At 1:30 p.m., the court reconvened out of the presence of the jury. Tim Ohms was the first to speak.

"I just learned at lunch that another federal agency obtained a search warrant, I believe this morning, for Mr. Stegeman's residence, which is also this defendant's residence. It is my understanding that they obtained the warrant in order to search for Mr. Stegeman's passport. I am informed of some of the items that were discovered during the course of that search, and I disclosed the nature of those items to Mr. Sanger."

In truth, Ohms knew about the search warrant before it was served.

"Of course, I knew in advance that they were going to search Stegeman's house, which was also the defendant's house, that day. It was something that came as a surprise to me, but I didn't have to tell Sager about it until the warrant was served," elaborated Ohms. "I was kind of in a bind, because it was an unusual situation. I was in no position to make any call as to what the defense could or would use on behalf of Barb Fraley. They are entitled to know anything and everything. For all I knew, Sanger wanted to use the results of the search to bolster his argument that Stegeman was the bad guy and Barb was his innocent victim. That is not for me to say, and I wanted to make sure Sanger knew exactly what was going on. I did not want to find myself in any sort of situation where the court could declare a mistrial."

Judge Van Sickle wasn't quite sure what was happening.

"All right. What do you see to do at this time?"

"Well, I want to place that on record because some of the information or material that was discovered would ordinarily have relevance to this case. I don't intend to introduce any evidence of that nature on rebuttal, because that wasn't the intent of the search in the first place."

Ohms felt it was important to notify Sanger of the incriminating evidence found during the search and wanted it on the record. He was not about to jeopardize his case or future prosecutions by making any errors.

Van Sickle turned to Sanger.

"Anything you wish to make known to the court at this time?"

"Your honor, as far as I know about what was discovered, it would be corroborative of the defense theory that Mr. Stegeman was the manufacturer of the bills."

However, if the new evidence also implicated Barb, he couldn't risk looking into it further.

"I don't know enough about it to ask for a continuance to explore it," said a weary Richard Sanger. "I don't know what I might run into. So, I believe at this point in time my best option is to proceed."

The jury was supplied instructions, verdict forms, and final arguments.

Then the deliberations began.

"Do you think the jury doesn't read the newspaper?"

The rhetorical question came from Richard Sanger, noting reporter Bill Morlin's ongoing coverage of Barb and Harold's legal misadventures in *The Spokesman-Review*. On the morning after Barb's final testimony, the following headline story appeared in the local paper:

FEDERAL AGENTS FIND SIGNS
OF COUNTERFEITING

"Thursday, as Barbara Fraley told a Spokane jury she didn't know anything about counterfeit money, federal agents searched her Hayden Lake, Idaho, home and said they found evidence of a counterfeiting operation," wrote Morlin. "The U.S. District Court jury wasn't told about the discovery made by Secret Service agents and a State Department investigator. The jury will resume its deliberations this morning to decide whether the forty-four-year-old mother of five is guilty of passing counterfeit money."

Richard Sanger rolled his eyes and leaned back in his creaking public-defender chair. There was barely room for disappointment in his cramped, windowless office.

"I have some real problems with the way the government handled this case."

FOURTEEN

What we are dealing with here is a matter of perception.
—Richard Sanger
Public Defender

Lyle Workman insisted that arresting Stegeman on the verge of Barb's trial was not planned as a prosecution tactic, but was the result of last-minute confirmation that Stegeman wasn't Stegeman.

"We didn't arrest Harold to impact Sanger's defense of Barb," explained Workman. "I just happened to come at a bad time for him, and he had his hands full as it was."

Sparks flew between Sanger and Workman during the trial. Both became visibly overheated during a pointed exchange in which Sanger implied that Workman withheld important information from the defense.

"This Harold Stegeman who's married to Barbara Fraley, he's been a very difficult person to check out as far as identity is concerned," began Sanger.

"Very difficult," responded Workman.

"Have you been able to find out who he really is?"

"No, sir."

Workman had already testified about the counterfeiting ingredients listed on the back of the Inland Photo Supply business card.

"Do you know what country he's a citizen of?"

continued Sanger.

"No, sir."

Sanger then blindsided Workman with an unexpected question.

"When did I first learn about the card and these other businesses and this identification?"

"I'm sorry?"

Sanger rephrased the question, tingeing it with blatant bile.

"When was I first informed about the card in Stegeman's wallet and the photo supply business and the identity problem?"

"I don't know. It was in my report," Workman replied.

"A report to me?"

"It's in my memorandum report."

"Well," Sanger started to steam, "when you and I discussed this case last Wednesday or Thursday in Mr. Ohms's office, I asked you, did I not, 'What about Mr. Stegeman? Haven't you checked him out?' And you wouldn't give me any answers! Isn't that correct?"

Lyle went bolt upright in his seat.

"You know that I referred you to Mr. Ohms!"

"When?" countered Sanger. "Last Wednesday? Last Thursday? As of that time, I didn't know anything about this stuff you just testified to, isn't that true?"

Sanger had cause for anger. Although Workman received Harold Stegeman's birth certificate on March 5, and Sanger was notified of that information on March 6, the day of Harold's arrest, Workman kept a separate file on Stegeman—a file containing information not shared with the defense until Stegeman was in custody.

"There was a separate file on Mr. Stegeman, and the information in Mr. Stegeman's file only relates to Mr. Stegeman," testified Workman. "It does not relate to this defendant."

The tidbits about Harold using Barb's car, Barb's

son, and the alias of Frank Wincheski when purchasing counterfeiting supplies were never added to Barb's file, nor were any other aspects of Workman's investigation into possible or confirmed criminal behavior by Harold Stegeman.

"Well," Workman later explained, "they were two separate investigations. The reason for not wanting to tell [Barb] or her counsel everything I knew about Stegeman was security. It was an active investigation into Stegeman; Fraley is Stegeman's wife. It was difficult and unusual. I can see why Sanger would misunderstand and get irritated, but I couldn't jeopardize an investigation into an ongoing conspiracy."

The post-trial drive from Spokane to Hayden Lake allowed the frazzled Ms. Fraley little time for emotional decompression. The jury was deliberating. Harold, or whoever he was, was behind bars, and Barb attempted to process revelations about her counterfeit spouse amidst the chaotic intracranial residue of a grueling courtroom experience. She arrived home to find Secret Service agents, a representative of the U.S. State Department, and local law enforcement personnel crawling all over her house.

No one searched he raisin box on the porch. It didn't matter. Barb had burned the last bills long ago.

FIFTEEN

The fishermen know that the sea is dangerous and the storm terrible, but they have never found these dangers sufficient reason for remaining ashore.

— Vincent Van Gogh

"**C**rime on the High Seas?" Phil laughed as if he thought it was funny. He didn't. Not that he was naïve, but he was honestly hoping that Raul's desire to acquire this particular craft had nothing to do with concealed contraband.

"Contraband deluxe," confirmed the caffeinated Norwegian, "about three million dollars worth. We'll stop off in the Everglades and unload it. You'll see; the boats will come and meet us." He said it as if he were talking about the weather.

Phil decided to drink rum.

"I was already in the middle of it, so what else could I do? I figured Raul had taken care of everything, so I might as well do my best to relax, wait out the voyage, and collect my money."

Phil drank and waited. Then, in the shallow waters off the Everglades, he heard the roar of cigarette boats blasting out of the swamp. Forty feet long and with high-powered engines capable of slicing saltwater at 120 miles per hour, they were smugglers' dream machines.

"These guys pulled up and we stopped. The water

was glassy and calm as it usually was in the gulf," recalled Champagne. "Then they went down in the hull and started crashing around. It sounded like they were ripping open crates. I leaned against the rail lookin' at the boats rafted together along the side and ignored the whole damn thing. They started moving whatever they were yankin' out of the hull into the cigarette boats. Didn't seem like very much of whatever it was to me."

Phil Champagne put his head in his hands.

"I should have seen it comin', but what did I know?"

As Phil sipped rum and watched the transaction, the Norwegian and the leader of the cigarette crew began having an altercation. Voices got louder It had something to do with money.

"I don't remember if anyone called out a warning. All I know is that gunfire erupted. *Jesus Christ!* Just what I needed. I dropped to my hands and knees. There was a steel rail all around the ship with scuppers under it. I remember thinking that I hoped the bullets didn't come under and hit me. I thought they were gonna murder us all sure as shit. The shooting went on, then stopped, and then I heard the roar of the boats taking off."

Phil expected to find his captain and crew in a blood-drenched pile. Nobody was even wounded.

"Yumpin' Yesus!" yelled the Norwegian. "They tried to kill us! I didn't bargain for this. Yumpin' Yesus!"

"Wait a second," barked Phil. "I don't know what you're gonna do, but let me get this straight: They took whatever that was and didn't pay for it, right?"

"Yeah."

"Christ! I'm glad my money isn't coming from there. We gotta tell Raul what happened."

They couldn't risk making a call from the ship's radio, and Phil was concerned that the gunshots had attracted the Coast Guard.

"If I were you," Phil said to the captain, "I'd turn this

thing around and get out of here."

Champagne took a good look in the direction of shore.

"Hell, that's Naples over there."

Naples, Florida, was homeland to the most astonishing trackers in history—the Seminole-Negroes. Their ancestors were runaway slaves who took refuge among the Florida Seminole. The Seminole were not a nomadic or predatory people, but sedentary and civilized; hunting was subordinate to stock-raising and farming. They only took to the warpath in self-defense. So did Phil Champagne. He knew nothing of Seminoles, the early development of Naples in 1885, or when the swamp buggy races became an October tradition. He only knew the best restaurants, cocktail lounges, and the phone number of one semi-regular lover.

If the Norwegian and the crew were working hand in glove with the gun-toting devils who absconded with the contraband, Phil wanted off the boat and immediately out of the game.

"We got a nice-sized Zodiac here," declared Phil. "I'm taking the son of a bitch and going to Naples."

And that is exactly what he did, running the Zodiac full tilt until it ran right up on the beach. Finding the beach was no problem; Naples has forty-one miles of public sand. Phil threw himself at the first phone booth he saw.

"Listen, honey, I'll do anything. I'll even marry you if you want, but I've got to get back to Ft. Lauderdale. Please let me borrow your car."

The odds of this particular dark-haired, thirty-five-year-old divorcee relinquishing her new silver 1985 Chevrolet Caprice Classic were remote in the extreme. She leased a new Chevy every year and babied it as some women do their poodles.

"Hell, no," said Phil's Gulf-side lover, "you're not borrowing my car. I'd rather go back to my first husband than let you even get behind the wheel. Besides," she paused, "you sound like you've been sucking rum all night. If we're going anywhere, it's together. You pay for munchies and gas both ways, and I'll drive."

And she did.

"We blasted that Chevy across what we used to call Alligator Alley, the cross-state highway."

She chain-smoked menthols and talked about pasta while Phil drank hot coffee and crunched his way through the greasy bag of chips they had snapped up at a convenience store.

"She always talked about pasta. If she ate all the pasta she talked about, she would've weighed 400 pounds, which, thank God, she didn't."

Phil's mind raced faster than the Chevy, computing the time lag between his departure and the ship's proposed arrival in Tampa Bay. How soon would Raul know? How fast could he get there? And, Phil wondered, what about Mike?

Phil had called Mike before the flight to Cayman, bragged about the "done deal" of two hundred grand, and proffered an invitation to a celebratory reunion.

"Give me a couple of days to make arrangements, pal," said Mike, "and don't get yourself into a jam. Remember, virtue is its own reward."

"I am, above all," insisted Champagne, "a virtuous man."

The reward Phil wanted was the $200,000. His virtue had always been generosity. The first would lead to the latter.

"When we reached Ft. Lauderdale and navigated to my moorage, I slid her gas money, a big kiss, and told her I would do something extra special for her someday. She was hoping to spend the night on the boat, but I told her that I would have to owe her one. "In fact," said Phil with a grin, "I still owe her one."

He got out of the car, walked down the ramp, onto the boat, and stopped dead in his tracks. Somebody was already on board. A shadow moved. Quick reasoning; no problem. One man had the key. Phil hadn't expected him to arrive another day or two, but he was happy to see him—Alias Mike.

"Man, you won't believe what happened," gasped Phil after grasping Mike's outstretched hand. "There was some sort of rip-off, and my buddy Raul doesn't even know yet."

Champagne hurriedly changed clothes, babbling details to Mike, who sat steely-eyed and intense. As an outsider, Mike soaked up the implications that washed over Phil's had.

"You know what you're going to do now?" asked Mike, who was about to tell Phil what to do.

"Damn right I know," interrupted Phil. "I'm cabbing it right over to Raul's place to let him know what happened, that I had nothing to do with it, and then arrange to get my $200,000."

Mike was incredulous.

"You're nuts!"

"Nuts?"

Mike stood up and poked a stubby finger into the center of Phil's chest. Mike was smaller, but his aura was stronger.

"Forget it. Forget Raul. Forget the $200,000." Each "forget" was punctuated by a poke. "Never call. Never go there. Never go back. Get the hell out of Florida. Period."

"Mike, you're so goddamn paranoid all the time," objected Phil as he grabbed Mike's finger. "Raul is my friend. I saved his life. In fact, I bet he gives me more than $200,000 because I'm tipping him off."

Phil believed it; Mike did not.

"Let go of my finger," Mike said.

Champagne splashed water on his face and poured himself a quick shot of vodka. There is, according to Phil, such a thing as a quick shot of vodka.

"I owe it to Raul to be straight-up with him. If I don't do this, he will for sure think I had something to do with it. You sit there, or go to the hotel. Either way, I'll be back as soon as I see Raul."

Mike pulled a .45 automatic out from under his coat as if it were a pocket watch.

"You want this, just in case?"

"Hey, this is Florida. I've got a couple of those myself. No offense, but I don't pack heat on social calls. I'm not taking a gun."

Then Peter ran off to play in Mr. McGregor's garden.

SIXTEEN

Human beings seem to have an almost unlimited capacity to deceive themselves, and to deceive themselves into taking their own lies for the truth.

—R. D. Laing

Jerry Fraley, Leanna Fraley, Richard Fraley Jr., and the recently arrived Barbara Fraley Stegeman watched the departing entourage of law enforcement officers. The dedicated protectors of America's currency handed over an itemized list of everything sized in the search, including the incriminating negatives, identification, passport, assorted catalogues, paper stocks, and scraps of note paper. Among the scraps was a lined sheet of lavender-colored paper with the following handwritten information: Gary Penar 922-2345.

"I am not an accomplice, I was not in the San Juans, and I am not a criminal," delineated Gary Penar. "I am an attorney who received a telephone call on March 6 from the magistrate's office indicating that they had an individual who was going to be testifying as a witness and they thought it would be a good idea to have him talk to an attorney before he testified. About an hour later I got a call from the same magistrate's office saying, 'He's no longer a witness; he's now been indicted. Do you still want to represent the guy?' I said, 'Sure.'"

Harold, however, wasn't so sure than Penar was

actually his defense attorney. His first suspicion was the Penar was a government agent pretending to be his lawyer to extract further information. After a session or two, Harold warmed up and soon intimated to Mr. Penar that he wasn't who he said he was.

"Hang on to your hat," advised Harold. "You're not going to believe this story."

Harold Stegeman then held up a yellow sheet of paper and pressed it against the glass separating the jailed defendant from his court-appointed attorney. Handwritten, for Penar's eyes only, were the astonishing details of the strange death and counterfeit resurrection of Phillip Wendell Champagne.

"When I read what he wrote, I about fell off my chair," admitted Penar. "Written out in longhand was an incredible tale about falling off a boat ten years earlier, people thinking he was dead, an ex-wife and four kids, changing identities in Florida. Jesus! I just rolled my eyes."

Phil, meanwhile, was becoming increasingly afraid.

"I feared being prosecuted for not saying that I knew I was alive. Because there was insurance paid out, I knew that everybody would say, 'Fraud, fraud, fraud,'" lamented Champagne. "That's what I was afraid of until I learned that the statute of limitations was up, and I couldn't and wouldn't be prosecuted for not being dead."

Phil also feared being charged with bank fraud.

"People were bound to figure that because I was living under another name that there had to be some intention to defraud the bank that lent me money for the restaurant. I paid back all those bank loans except the last one. The only reason the last one didn't get paid off was because I went bankrupt. Going bankrupt under an assumed name does not, under our current justice system, meet all of the legal requirements for a legitimate bankruptcy."

"If bank fraud were the only charge against me, I

would have gone to a jury trial. I never defrauded the bank, never intended to defraud the bank, and paid back every cent of every loan right up to the last. But, as I was facing counterfeiting charges, I was rather in a bind. Plus, poor, dear Barb..." Phil got misty at the thought of Barb's courtroom distress. "She was in one room of the courthouse defending herself while I was in another room of the same courthouse to be arraigned."

Harold entered a plea of not guilty; Penar argued, to no avail, for his release.

"At that point, things were very confusing," recalled Penar. "Nobody knew who he was. They thought he was either some fellow who died in a scuba accident in the Bahamas or a British mercenary who hung out off the coast of India or a missing drug dealer/informant named Ron Kollister."

The aforementioned British mercenary, allegedly affiliated with a New York crime family and responsible for agitation in the Maldive Islands, earned his place in the mix by traveling under the alias John L Stegeman. One Stegeman is as good as another, especially if the identification is false.

"There was a point," affirmed Lyle Workman, "when I was ready to see if I could get the Secret Service to spring for me to go show Harold's picture to David Joel Friedland to see if he would say, 'Oh, yeah, I remember that guy. We used to go scuba diving together in the Cayman and Maldive Islands.' I really thought that the common ground between all these Stegemans—Friedland, the mercenary, and our Harold—was going to be drug smuggling simply because of the Miami connection."

Drug smuggling was not, according to Agent Tom Sommero, a standard component of Friedland's criminal repertoire, although Sommero acknowledged Friedland was heavily scrutinized for involvement in a variety of Florida-based insurance frauds and one rather dicey incident involving counterfeit currency.

"The samples were great; the final product was lousy," remarked Sommero, who exonerated Phil Champagne from any direct association with either Friedland or the mercenary who traveled under a Costa Rican passport.

"It is, astonishingly enough, coincidence. The Stegeman who turned up on the West Coast (Phil Champagne) had the misfortune to acquire an alias already being used by organized crime."

Neither the FBI nor Interpol ever located the elusive British mercenary, nor did they figure out the true identity of the Harold Stegeman married to Barbara Fraley. A frustrated Lyle Workman took Stegeman's fingerprints to the local Spokane Police Department. They ran a standard five-state computer check. No problem.

"Here you go, Mr. Workman. The man's name is Phillip W. Champagne."

"Criminal record?" Lyle couldn't wait to hear the juicy details.

"Well, see for yourself. Nothing for the past forty years, not even a traffic citation."

Nothing for the past forty years.

Nothing.

"I couldn't figure out why this guy Phil Champagne was so reticent about revealing his true identity," recalled Workman "The last time he was in any trouble was way back in about 1952, and that was for taking a car without permission. What could have to hide?"

Being dead, for one thing.

Barb believed she would be found innocent. She really did.

"If the jury could only see that I was a victim. It was so obvious. I had always been a victim. How could someone who was such a good mother, such a hard worker, such a tender-hearted soul possibly be considered a criminal?"

"I had to believe I would be found innocent, simply because I was innocent," recalled Mrs. Stegeman, "but the jury judged me guilty. They sent me home to await sentencing.

"On May 15, 1992, I was sentenced to ten months in Geiger Corrections Center in Spokane, Washington, and two years probation. Mr. Sanger assured me that I would receive credit for the time I served on his monitor."

Sanger fought for that all the way to the Ninth Circuit Court of Appeals, but Barb never received credit for time spent on home monitor device.

SEVENTEEN

One would think that near relations, who live constantly together, and always have done so, must be pretty well acquainted with one another's characters. They are nearly in the dark about it.

—William Hazlitt

Barb, *sans* Harold, sat home with Jerry and Leanna; Harold sat in the Spokane County Jail. At the March 30 hearing, Timothy Ohms appeared on behalf of the United States while Gary Penar again represented Harold Richard Stegeman. As the defendant and his counsel walked into the courtroom, Tim Ohms pulled Penar aside.

"Well, we think we know for sure who he is."

Big deal. Penar already knew.

"I argued that Mr. Stegeman had opportunity and incentive to flee after the November arrest, but he did not flee. In addition," Penar noted, "Harold had ties to the community and opportunity for employment at Haden Lake, Therefore, I reasoned, Mr. Stegeman need not be detained."

Timothy Ohms contended that Harold's identity was still not known.

"He may be Phil Champagne, gentleman crook to the Secret Service," stated Monte Le Hew, owner of the infamous doghouse hideaway of Stegeman's bogus bills, "but he will always be good ol' Harold to me. He was always wonderful to Barb's kids and treated her like she was gold-plated. He was, and is, a real nice guy."

Phil's original family were admittedly stunned to discover that not only was he alive, but he was behind bars.

"I kept telling Phil that he had better call and talk to his kids," said Barb, "but he was afraid of what they might say to him. His daughter Renee called me when I was in Hayden Lake on the home monitor awaiting sentencing She called me and said, 'I don't know how to say this, but I'm Phil's daughter.'"

Phil screwed up his courage and called Kathy and Renee at Kathy's house in Portland. Kathy wouldn't talk, but Renee was eager to hear her father's voice.

"I don't remember what was said word for word, except that I would try to explain sometime why I did what I did. Renee said, 'I don't care about explanations. I understand. I'm just glad that you're alive.'"

Barb had to put all of her household goods in storage, find a secure home for her two minor children, and emotionally prepare herself for imprisonment.

"I had not had any luck finding anyone to take my youngest girl, and then Renee came to the rescue. She and her husband offered to take care of Leanna for the full ten months of my sentence. They were wonderful to all of us, supportive in so many ways."

Phil Champagne doesn't stint on his expressions of appreciation either.

"Anytime we needed anything, we could depend on Renee and her husband, Steve. They certainly have my praise and appreciation. They stood by me, Barb, and did everything they could to help."

Despite Phil penning a written apology entreating their patience and understanding, the remaining Champagne children stayed immeasurably aloof.

"I really didn't want the kids to come see me in jail. It would be too humiliating. I was embarrassed enough, shamed enough, as it was. I don't think Mitch was too eager to see me, not with Federal Kemper hounding him to return the money they paid out. For a long time, I couldn't bring myself to even think about poor John Robin having been blamed all these years for my death, now knowing that I was alive."

John Robin heard of Phil's resurrection from Ed Grass, who saw it in the newspaper.

"I said, "Get me a copy of that paper,' then I called Mitch and he said that he had heard from Phil and it was true. At first, I thought it had to be a mistake. I couldn't see any way that he could have survived. I retraced my steps a thousand times to see where I went wrong, what I could have done to save him. Maybe he swam in the wrong direction. Perhaps he swam toward lights that were farther away. I don't know. But when I first heard that he was alive, I thought it couldn't be true."

EIGHTEEN

*The fear of death is the most unjustified of all fears, for
there's no risk of accident to someone who's dead.*

—Albert Einstein

"**H**ey man, I'm lucky to be alive," said Phil.
"Not for long, you stupid gringo," growled
Raul.

It was not the welcome Phil had anticipated.
Banging on Raul's door, he was initially greeted with
friendly surprise from his good buddy and two Hispanic
gentlemen Phil had met at the party.

"How did you get here so soon? Come in and tell me
what happened."

Phil asked if anyone had contacted Raul about
anything. The answer was negative in the extreme.

"When I told him about the guys taking the goods,
shooting their guns, and all that, he changed. He became
totally different, and all three of them started talking in
Spanish. They were very excited."

Raul invited Phil into the kitchen for a drink and
conversation.

"The reason I want you to come in the kitchen,"
explained Raul as Phil looked for evidence of refreshment
or hospitality, "is so you won't bleed all over my carpet."

Bleed?

There was a gun at Phil's head. Not a big gun, but a

gun nonetheless.

"Sit in that chair and stay there, you dumb gringo, or I'll blow your fucking head off."

Phil sat down. If there was ever a time for Champagne to pour on the charm, this had to be it. Charm, however, is difficult when you are losing control of your bladder.

"What's wrong?" entreated Phil. "Do you think I took your goods?"

"Shut up! You're so dumb, you couldn't steal anything from me! You're supposed to be dead!"

Raul didn't know the half of it. Phil, perceptive in the face of certain death, chose pleading as a viable option

"I thought you were my friend. You said we were brothers. You said that was the Cuban way," simpered Phil, his knees knocking together like boney castanets.

"Cuban? Did I say I was Cuban?" You're so stupid! I'm not Cuban. They're not Cuban. For all you know, we could be from Mexico, Honduras, Peru, Colombia, Panama, or from the goddamn state of Texas! It's a good thing you're in the kitchen," reaffirmed Raul. "I can clean the blood off the tile."

It was beginning to look as if Raul's "good friend, Peter Donovan" was not going to get the $200,000.

"For Christ's sake," pleaded Phil, "what have I ever done to you?"

"For one thing," Raul replied, "you fucked my sister."

Perhaps Raul needed personal boundary clarification, but Phil sensed it was not the time to recommend professional counseling.

"I knew my number was up for sure. Raul was ranting and raving about how all of us on the boat were supposed to be dead. Apparently, the guys in the cigarette boats were supposed to kill us all, take the stuff, and leave the boat adrift. Don't ask me why. They didn't kill anybody, so Raul was doubly pissed. He said at least he would have the pleasure of killing me himself. I was so scared, I almost passed out. I forced myself to think about my situation. The only chance I could see was the large window to my right. I figured I might be able to throw myself against it with enough force to go through. I would probably get cut to ribbons, but I might survive."

One of the three was on the telephone. From what Phil understood with his limited grasp of Spanish, they needed to either know something or get permission before they could shoot him.

"I wasn't clear on the exact nature of the conversation, except that it was highly animated and involved me. Maybe they were discussing a good place to dump the body. I was in shock and everyone seemed to move in slow motion. I sat like a pasty-faced statue, hardly moving a muscle, watching as one of Raul's henchmen pointed the gun around the room. I imagine that had it been a movie, I would have jumped up and kicked the shit out of all of 'em, because they weren't holding the gun on me like I was someone they were really afraid of."

Phil turned slightly to get his feet under himself so he could take a life or death lunge at the glass. He didn't take the lunge; he took a look. Through the window, beyond the glare and darkness, was Alias Mike.

"The one guy was off the phone, but the three men were still talking in Spanish and very involved in what they were saying. Knowing I was helpless, they paid almost no attention to me as long as I just sat in the chair. I could see Mike making a questioning motion, so when they weren't looking, I ran my finger quickly across my throat in a gesture that anyone would understand. In an instant, Mike was gone."

Ding-dong. Back doorbell.

The air was ice.

Raul put his finger to his lips and lowered the gun to his side They all looked at the door. Raul faked a cheery voice.

"Un momento, por favor."

Raul cautiously turned the doorknob and opened the door a crack to see who was there.

WHAM!

The door burst open with such swift and sudden violence it was as if the room warped into a grainy late-show reality. Standing rock solid in the kicked-open doorway leveling an automatic with deadly accuracy was Alias Mike.

In fiction, they call it a dramatic pause. In fact, it was an instant. Six deafening rounds of chaos and cordite roared in the tiled kitchen, three bodies jerked, shuddered, and thudded to the floor.

"Raul was the first to be hit. The next two got it in rapid succession. They were all hit a second time by the three shots that immediately followed. It was deafening—BOOM! BOOM! BOOM! BOOM! BOOM! BOOM! They were all dead before they fell."

Phil and Mike got the hell out as fast as they could, walking rapidly toward the main highway and the busier area. If anyone had heard the shots, their reaction was not immediate. No one paid any attention to the two gentlemen out for a stroll.

"We made it to a store with an outside phone and called a cab and made it back to the boat. Mike took a rat-tail file and ran it down the barrel of the gun. He filed the hell out of the firing pin and washed his hands with chlorine bleach. Then he disassembled the gun and threw it in one of the canals."

Back at the boat, Mike decided to call another cab, return to his hotel, and fly back to the Northwest with his pilot ex-relative. Before leaving, he gave Phil one last piece of advice.

"I strongly suggest you get the hell out of town, and do it now," Mike said as he packed a few remaining items. "Call me in a few days and let me know that you're still alive."

Alone on the boat, Phil poured himself a drink. His legs were still shaking. Three dead. Crime on the high seas. Two-hundred thousand dollars sitting in a banker's box at Raul's ranch.

And then Phillip Wendell Champagne had a flash of either insanity or inspiration. The audacity of the idea and the giddy improbability were incapable of withstanding logical scrutiny, but Phil had abandoned logical scrutiny the night he fell off John Robin's boat.

Phil banged the glass on the table, went to a drawer, and took out a gun. There was $200,000 in a dead man's safe somewhere over the Georgia border with Peter Donovan's name on it. This was it, the moment of truth. There was only one way he could pull it off, and he was determined to try. Phil loaded the gun and scrambled through his address book for a phone number.

"Hey, listen, this is Peter Donovan …Yeah, fine. … Listen, I've got an emergency. I need your help and I need it now. You're the only guy I can turn to, the only one who can help me. …Yeah. You bet. I'm on my way."

Champagne pocketed the gun, grabbed his checkbook, and hailed a cab.

Damn! said Phil to himself, *that money is mine and I'm gonna get it!*

NINETEEN

I takes a sharp observer to tell innocence from assurance.
—Charles Dudley Warner

The ammo loaded by the United States government for use against Phil Champagne was, for both Gary Penar and his client, too powerful to ignore.

"After Barb was found guilty and her sentencing came down, Phil knew he was in for a rough time," noted Penar.

"They had him pretty clean on the counterfeiting charge. I think Phil decided to cooperate early on. He was sort of glad that the ruse was over."

Lyle Workman and Timothy Ohms had no interest in locking up Phil Champagne and throwing away the key, quite the contrary. As do most people, Lyle and Tim took a liking to the former Mr. Stegeman.

"The approach we were coming from was not that we wanted Phil to do hard time. We just wanted to make sure we got all the money and all the plates. We wanted to get to the bottom of this thing."

Champagne and Penar decided to cut a deal. Phil would plead guilty to anything and everything they wanted to toss at him, and he would take the role as mastermind of a criminal organization, tell them absolutely everything in detail, and make sure they recovered every possible bill, plate, or trace of his counterfeiting operation. The government, in return, would recommend to the court that Phil receive the minimum sentence and agree not to pursue any further charges against Barb, Monte LeHew, Richard Fraley Jr., Danny LeHew, or Monte's dog. In short, if Phil told everything, olly-olly oxen free.

"We promised to cooperate fully with the government," confirmed Penar, "and we did; we showed them where things were buried in the woods. As part of the agreement, they brought in a polygraph operated by a guy out from San Francisco. They set it up at the Spokane County Jail, hooked Phil up to it then asked him all sorts of questions to make sure he was telling the truth. I got tired of hanging around, and they kind of asked me to leave anyway, so I told Phil that if there was any problem or any question he didn't feel comfortable with, to give me a call."

Two hours later, Phil called.

"Gary, I got a problem here."

"What's that, Phil?"

"Did I ever tell you about the twenties?"

"Twenties?" Gary paused. "No, Phil, you never told me anything about twenties."

"Oh. Well, I guess you should know that I also made a stack of twenty-dollar bills. I never passed any. No one ever passed any, but I made them."

Once again, they traipsed out to the woods and dug up the remnants of the twenty-dollar plates.

Phil laughed when he heard the story recounted.

"Yeah, I made twenty-dollar bills, but they looked pretty bad and felt worse. The only way you could ever pass one would be to hand it to a blind drunk who had a bag over his head and was wearing heavy gloves. I tried all manner of denominations as test runs. I just forgot to tell Gary about those."

Penar regarded Champagne as one of his more delightfully entertaining clients.

"The one thing about Phil that bothers me is this: If he had put the same effort into a legitimate enterprise, he would have made a lot more money. My impression of Phil is that he got in over his head, had an unpleasant situation he could no longer deal with, and took off to have a new life. Had he resisted the temptation to counterfeit, he probably could have gone on the rest of his life without ever being 'caught.' He could have lived out the rest of his days as Harold Stegeman. But he made a decision to go for what looked like easy money. But it wasn't easy, and it wasn't real."

The Maltese Falcon also wasn't real, but unlike Sam Spade, Phil Champagne was willing to take the fall and play the sap. Barb still insisted she was innocent. Phil still insisted she wasn't. Interestingly, this was not a source of conflict between them. Her denial and his affirmation served the same purpose—protecting Barb. Although she was found guilty of passing bad bills, Phil may have feared additional charges would be made against her once the extent of the counterfeiting operation was known.

"Phil promised to tell us the truth," affirmed Lyle Workman, "and he told us that Barb was in on it almost from the get-go. I believe him one hundred percent. But hypothetically speaking—and I do mean hypothetically—if Barb was innocent and Phil feared that we would prosecute her for conspiracy to manufacture, if he didn't say she was guilty, it might make sense to him to implicate her in order to protect her. The truth of the matter is that we would not have gone after her anymore than we already had. But if in his mind he imagined that the only way for her to be protected from future charges was for him to say she was guilty, he would certainly take that position. After all, it was because of Phil's cooperation that we never went after Monte LeHew or Richard Fraley Jr. So, by saying Barb was in on it, she would be safe."

Far-fetched? Certainly. Neither Lyle Workman nor Tim Ohms bought it for a minute, but few aspects of Phil's story have been anywhere within the bounds of basic rationality. Such was the case when Phil found himself flying several thousand feet above Georgia.

TWENTY

It is by surprise that experience teaches all she designs to teach us.

—Charles Sander Pierce

"I know right where we're going. Just follow the river," advised Phil.

"Gotcha, pal," said Stretch. "I just wish we had a helicopter so we could set down. I don't know what you're into, Pete, but I'd be right there with ya, both guns blazin'."

There are people in this world who will jump at adventure without a second thought. In fact, the very act of jumping is their first thought. When Phil took his first static line jump with some friends from Ft. Lauderdale, Stretch was piloting the plane. It was Stretch who became his occasional drinking buddy, and Stretch who was always a wink and a nod away from illegality. Stretch had a plane, accepted checks from people he knew, and didn't ask questions. Phil wrote Stretch a perfectly good check for $2,500 to put him in a parachute, fly him over Raul's ranch, and toss him out of the plane.

"I'm sorry to get you up at this time of the morning, Stretch, but it's urgent," explained Phil when he showed up at Stretch's trailer at an ungodly hour of the morning. "I know that if I were a woman, you wouldn't mind."

"Hey, it's okay. It's okay," Stretch assured him. "What's happening? What do ya need?"

"Listen, I'm in a lot of trouble. I've got to go up over the border into Georgia, and I gotta get there before anybody else does. I'm willing to pay. I think the only way I can get into where I'm going is to jump. I know you're into this shit, so I bet you can get me a parachute, and we can pull this off."

Stretch lit up like Gabby Hayes in an old "B" Western movie.

"If you need some help, I got a couple buddies who have automatic weapons. We can go get them."

"No, I've got a gun, but I don't think I'll need it. All I gotta do is get there, grab something, and get the hell out."

Stretch started pulling things together.

"I can get everything you need in fifteen minutes," insisted Stretch when Phil told him that he would pay $2,600. "I'll take the money, but I'd do it just for the fun of it. This is my kind of job. But you won't have to jump if I can set down. Honest, I can land my plane on a dime. Then I can fly you out."

Phil wished it could be that way, but he knew that without a helicopter, there was no way to land.

"I think the plane was a Cessna 185," said Champagne, doing his best to remember details, "but where the doors open on the right-hand side, most airplanes have a little door you open so you can climb in the back or the front. Well, this had been cut out and it had a door that folded up to the wing and fastened and dropped down. Stretch said it was for skydiving and 'dropping other things.' The way it worked was simple. You step out on the side, put a foot on that thing, and then the step went out to the wing. You just grab hold of the hand-holds and go when you're gonna go."

For one brief moment prior to take off, Phil almost

came to his senses and gave it up. The moment passed, and at 7:45 a.m., the two men took off into the Florida skies.

"Stretch was familiar with the area, and when I described the terrain I saw the first time I flew up with Raul, he knew what I was talking about. We flew, refueled once, and then kept on going. I easily found the place. It was no trouble at all. Different things went through my mind, like, 'What if I can't find it?' But we found it easy enough."

There was the river. It all looked familiar.

"Follow that turn, keep going, look for the next turn in the river...," Phil directed.

Phil figured the chances were good that no one could have moved fast enough to beat him to the ranch.

"We flew over the house at thirty-five hundred feet, checking it out for cars or helicopters that would have told me if anyone was there."

No helicopter, no car, not even the caretaker's pickup.

Phil mused out loud, as they circled overhead, "Not a soul is home, not even servants. I don't think anyone is there at all."

"I see a good place to set down," Stretch interrupted, "but it would be a lot easier if we had a chopper. If there's anyone to see you, they might see you when you jump."

"Jesus, Stretch, I didn't exactly have a lot of time to plan this. I'm just gonna jump and take my chances."

Stretch circled several miles from the house, bringing the plan to exactly twenty-five hundred feet.

I'll tell you when to go. If I could, I would go with you, you know I would."

Phil opened the door.

"I never once thought of changing my mind and going back. At that moment, I knew I was a different person than I had been a few years earlier."

Stretch wished Pete all the luck in the world. Knowing

he'd need it, Phil accepted the wish.

Champagne jumped, and the earth rushed up to meet him.

"I never saw Stretch again, but I made sure his check cleared the bank before I closed out the account," said Phil. "I wanted to make sure he got paid in full."

When Phil finally came back to earth, he landed in a field of tall grass a quarter mile from the house. He folded the chute, took off his jump gear, hid the stuff in nearby bushes, and waited to see if anyone had noticed him.

"I made my way through the pasture, open land, deep grass, hedgerows, and those pine woods. As I crept toward the house, the dogs came rushing at me, barking like crazy, until they realized that they knew me. I calmed them down, because I knew that if there was someone inside the house, all that dog noise would bring 'em out."

Phil heard a door open. He crouched in the bushes and waited. Sure enough, someone was in the house and had stepped out to the patio to see why the dogs were barking.

I'll be damned, Phil said to himself. *I know that guy.* Phil was pissed.

He had risked life and limb for the box of loot only to find there was an unexpected houseguest at Raul's country estate. The mystery guest wasn't one of Raul's regular buddies, nor was he someone Phil Champagne had seen in Florida before. He was a familiar face from days gone by.

"I moved around the house and peered in the window," explained Champagne. "I couldn't see anyone else inside. When I heard him return to the house, I carefully moved back toward the patio, slid up alongside the patio door, and looked in. He was watching television with his back to me."

Phil decided to take the direct approach and rely on

the element of surprise. He pulled out his .45 and took a deep breath.

"I walked through those French doors like I was Alan Ladd; that son of a bitch almost soiled his shorts when he saw me standing there with my automatic aimed at his heart. I hoped he couldn't tell how bad my hands were shaking."

The startled occupant froze in fear, his eyes fixed in stark terror. What he was seeing was impossible but true—Peter Donovan had come back from the dead.

Again.

"Stick 'em up," growled Phil. "Reach for the sky."

TWENTY-ONE

But the kind of deceit that is treachery is quite another matter.
　　—Julian Jaynes, *The Origin of Consciousness in the Breakdown of the Bicameral Mind*

The man in Phil's sights made a feeble attempt to stand and then an equally inept foray into the world of babbling explanations.

"Sit down and shut up!" ordered Phil. "What do you know about Raul?"

"He's ... he's dead ... and two others," stammered he trembling captive. "They found the bodies ... no one knows who ... why ... no cops ... can't afford ..."

Phil cut him off with a glare and a gesture.

"You know who blew them away? Me! I did it," lied tough guy Champagne. Having the upper hand, Phil felt entitled to play the badass. "Now how about you? You wanna try something? Feel lucky? Well, do ya, punk?" Phil said with bravado.

"I was probably as scared as he was," remembered Champagne, "But I had a gun; he didn't. Plus I was mad as hell. After all, this jerk was the same one who stood on the dock at Cancun and motioned to the guys with the high-powered rifles to blow Sam and me away. The son of a bitch had tried to kill me, for God's sake."

Any machismo left in the icy veins of the fearful

fellow cowering in the chair evaporated in the heat of the moment. It was the bad guy's turn to plead for mercy

"I'll tell you whatever you want to know, honest. I was only following orders," whimpered Miguel.

"Go on," prompted Phil, "let's hear it."

"When you first came to Merida, I called Raul and asked him what to do. You knew all the passwords, but I didn't trust you; there was something funny about you. I thought you were a Fed or some kind of a special agent. We already figured that Sam was a snitch. Raul told me to make you think you were in, then get rid of you."

"Ya missed, stupid," Phil added with disdain, "and you shot up a perfectly good boat." Phil liked rubbing it in.

"Then," continued Miguel, "a long time later, I saw you at a nightclub here in Florida. At first, I was afraid you'd seen me. After a while, I knew you hadn't. I called Raul, and he came to the club to take a look."

"And?"

"Can I put my hands down?" asked Miguel hopefully.

"No. You can shove them up your ass or put them on the top of your head, whichever is more comfortable."

Miguel put his hands atop his head and continued.

"When Raul arrived, you were doing your German act for your friends. He told me to stay out of sight and said, 'We can use this dummy to cure our problem in the Cayman Islands.'"

Dummy?

"Yumpin' Yesus," intoned Phil as he shifted his weight and re-leveled his .45. "You mean the whole damn thing about the scuba diving accident and saving his life was a setup? What a bunch of dirty, stinking bastards."

Phil sat down wearily behind Raul's desk, resting his right elbow from the weight of the gun, and stared at the nattily dressed but profusely perspiring criminal. The man looked empty, shrunken, and impotent. The only sound in the room came from the television. An attorney was advertising his services for victims of wrongful death or personal injury.

"They thought I was some sort of goddamn Lyle Workman," recounted Phil with a bemused laugh. "I guess they could tell there was something unusual about me, that I had something to hide, but all I was hiding was that I was supposed to be dead. Once this jerk laid it all out for me, it seemed pretty damn transparent. After all, when I was in Cancun, he told me that he wanted me to deliver that sailboat to Marathon. I had put that whole awful episode out of my mind, so I never even thought of there being any connection between my nightmare in Mexico and my good buddy Raul, may he rot in Hell."

Phil popped open the panel and took out the box. It was all still there—the money and the note. Peter Donovan read it aloud.

"See?" said Phil when he was done reading, "I'm just here to claim what's mine."

"What about me?" Miguel was desperate.

You don't get any," joked Phil. "You don't deserve a cent."

That was not what Miguel had meant.

"You're going to kill me," he said, as if announcing a ball score. "Fuck you, then. Get it over with."

Phil Champagne did not intend to kill anyone.

"For God's sake, all you lowlifes know how to do is zip each other off and shoot people. I swear, you give criminals a bad name. All I'm gonna do is tie you up and walk away. I let you live; you never say a word. That's the deal. You never saw me; I never saw you."

Maybe Miguel saw the last meaningless minutes of his life washing away on the red mist rolling over his eyes. He had told men that they were not going to die knowing full well that they would soon be bloodied, lifeless, and stuffed in the trunk of a car or weighted to the bottom of the ocean. Perhaps his internal mental projector played back every incident of mayhem and carnage, which he had dispassionately directed. Perhaps not.

For whatever reasons, fueled by whatever emotions, Miguel failed to believe the promise of the man known to him as Peter Donovan. Miguel decided that if he was going to die, he would go down fighting. All he needed was an opportunity. He knew exactly which drawer of Raul's desk contained a loaded .38 revolver.

Phil stood up with the banker's box under his left arm and moved away from the desk. He was looking for something to restrain the increasingly distraught Miguel. He walked across the room and turned off the television, terminating the irritating sales pitch for audiocassettes on how to get rich in real state. With the television off, Phil heard the distinctive rumble of the caretaker's pickup coming down the road.

Champagne glanced from Miguel to the window and back. Miguel was out of the chair.

"Stop!" yelled Phil. "Stop, goddamn it!"

Miguel lunged over the desktop, threw open the top right drawer, and spun around clutching a .38 revolver.

"Don't!"

He did.

"I'll be damned if the son of a bitch didn't try to kill me again," said Champagne "I could have shot him anytime, but I wouldn't. And there he is in a hot sweat panic lying sideways across Raul's desk pointing that .38 right at me. The little prick even pulled the trigger. Scared the hell out of me."

The shot went wild, but for all Phil knew, Miguel had shot him. All he heard was gunfire, round after round. All except the first came from the .45.

"I felt my gun going off in my hand. Once, twice, then again. I was firing out of fear and reflex; I wasn't aiming."

Bullets slammed into the wood desk right by Miguel, splinters flew everywhere, and he went flailing off to the right. The crack when his head hit the table was almost as loud as the gunfire.

His gun did a loop-de-loop and plopped on the carpet.

Miguel's limp body lay against the wall on the opposite side of the desk by the coffee table, but Phil saw no bloodstains.

"The dumb shit either knocked himself out cold by hitting his head on that coffee table, or he fainted out of sheer fright. Maybe the little prick had a well-deserved heart attack. I don't know and I don't really care. I would have been perfectly happy to have shot him, but I don't have Mike's aim or Mike's nerve."

Phil was not about to give CPR or call 911; he headed for the breezeway. His ride had arrived.

"They had just stopped the truck by the carport and the two of them had stepped out when I showed up brandishing that .45. I said, 'Go on, move, I'm borrowing the truck,' and I used my most gruff and commanding voice."

One of the caretakers turned and ran toward the back of the house. The other followed, so Phil took time to unload the groceries before driving away.

"Yes, I unloaded their groceries," said Champagne with a hearty laugh. "I guess I figured they needed them. I don't know. You do strange things when you've just been in a gunfight."

Phil and his $200,000 cruised twenty miles from where Raul's road turned off from the secondary highway. He ditched the pickup and caught a bus to a larger city where he caught another bus to Miami. The .45 eventually wound up in the bottom of a swamp, and Phil, still clutching the box, rode a taxi back to his boat in Ft. Lauderdale.

"I thought, *What the hell*. I knew it could be

dangerous, but I had gone so far already. I grabbed what belongings I needed and checked into a motel. The next day I called a boat broker with a story about how I had to move it fast, preferably for cash, and I was willing to sell it at a greatly reduced price."

In the best of scenarios, the broker would have found a wealthy character in Ft. Lauderdale eager to fork over hard cash for huge savings. Phil's life was seldom the best of scenarios. The broker found an eager buyer in Tampa. Phil would have to deliver the boat and take a check.

Checking accounts had been driving Phil crazy ever since he returned from Georgia. When a man has over $200,000 in cash—there was more than the promised amount in the box—he has to put it somewhere.

"I opened so many checking accounts at so many different branches under so many different names, it was hard to keep track," remembered the man of a thousand monikers. "I would deposit a few thousand more in cash every day, then write myself checks to move the money around. I always made sure they were noninterest bearing accounts so there were no problems."

What Phil Champagne needed was a new identity, not just another phony name. He needed a birth certificate, driver's license, Social Security number, and a U.S. passport. He needed to become someone solid.

Harold Richard Stegeman was the perfect someone.

"I had been checking into this new identity business, because I knew that once I had an established identity, I could put all the money into interest-bearing accounts or CDs, pay my taxes like a good American, and go somewhere and lead a normal life. I picked out Harold Stegeman as my new identity after visiting several graveyards Hell, with the boat sold, I had enough to retire."

Phil represented himself as acting on behalf of

relatives interested in documenting the Stegeman family history and paid the required fee for little Harold's birth certificate. The birth certificate enabled Phil to acquire a Social Security number. He then manufactured a Cayman Islands driver's license and resident permit, which, in conjunction with the birth certificate, allowed him to obtain a real Florida license.

"I took the driver's test and they never asked me for any other identification, even though I had it on me just in case."

Armed with all manner of authentic and fraudulent identification, securing the U.S. passport was no problem. It wasn't legal, but it worked.

"I opened a checking account at the Pinellas Park branch of NCNB, took the boat to Tampa, and got paid $105,000. The buyer paid the broker, and the broker, after deducting his commission, wrote a check to the corporation that owned the boat."

As the finances were becoming complicated, Phil turned to the Tampa attorney who set up his ownership of the boat in the first place, the same attorney who represented his ex-flame, Ann.

"I simply endorsed that check over to the attorney. He then issued two checks. Let's say on was to Don Carlson and one was to Joe Cook. As I was them," explained Phil with adolescent laughter, "I endorsed them over to Harold Richard Stegeman and made a deposit. Then I started writing myself checks out of my other accounts, too. As I had a real Social Security number, I was able to invest that money in CDs and earn interest. It didn't take long before all my money was in the name of Harold Stegeman."

Armed with an NCNB Checkmate Visa debit card, Harold Stegeman had immediate ATM access to over $300,000, petty cash in his pocket, and a bright future ahead of him. He bought a new travel trailer and pointed it west.

"I've got it made," thought Harold. "I've got a real name and plenty of money. Now all I need is a nice quiet town with nice quiet people. Hell, if I pick the right spot, build a house, maybe open a little business, no one will hardly even know I'm there."

Of all the places on Earth, Harold picked Shelton.

"I can't give you a good reason why I picked Shelton," admitted Champagne, "except that maybe in the back of my mind I was hoping to be seen, to somehow have it be known that I was alive."

As true as the maxim, "Wherever you go, there you are," is the corollary, "Wherever you are is where you were going.

Phil went to prison.

The phrase "bank fraud" does not have a nice ring to it. No need to ask for whom the bell tolls; the Feds were ringing up new charges against Phil Champagne.

Phil pleaded guilty to swearing falsely in a bankruptcy court action in 1989 and lying on his application for a bank loan in 1988. The lie was being Harold Stegeman when he borrowed $5,000 from Puget Sound Bank in Shelton, then listing that loan as a debt in his bankruptcy filing the next year. A Seattle judge imposed an additional six months to Champagne's sentence.

"Under my deal with the government, I pleaded guilty to everything," acknowledged Champagne. "I also pleaded guilty to a federal charge filed in Florida accusing me of making false statements in an application for a U.S. passport."

Prosecuting Attorney Rolf Tangvald offered his observations and recommendations concerning appropriate punishment in the passport case.

"Sentencing in this can involve anything from zero

to five years in prison, one to five years probation, and up to a $2,000 fine. The government is recommending that the low end of the sentence be imposed. The reason is that we would like to assist Mr. Champagne in getting his criminal past cleaned up. It was not the intention of either the government or of the defense counsel to impose additional sentence upon him."

The court agreed, added no further jail time to Phil's sentence, but charged a $100 special assessment. Wisely, Phil did not pay it with money from under Monte LeHew's doghouse

It could have been worse. Prosecutor Rolf Tangvald contacted Seattle Postal Inspector Mike Parry requesting help to develop a viable conspiracy and mail fraud case from the 1982 accident and Federal Kemper's subsequent payment to Mitch Champagne. In May 1992, as part of the investigation, Inspector Parry and sheriff's Detective Brent Cornwall traveled to Boise Idaho, for a little chat with Larry Wills.

"It was like he had seen a ghost," recalled Parry. Wills had read of Phil's survival and was not particularly thrilled about the implications. If Phil's fall from the *Warlock* was no accident, if the whole thing was a scam, Wills could be the most important and least questioned player in the game. Wills steadfastly clung to his original statements. If the Champagne brothers had faked Phil's death, Larry Wills believed he had also been deceived "to add credibility" to the nights' events. Wills cut short his interview with Parry and Cornwall, reiterating his complete innocence of any complicity in suspected wrongdoing.

Undaunted, Postal Inspector Parry continued the mundane task of developing a mail fraud case while the prosecuting attorneys pondered a puzzling legal conundrum: Had the statute of limitation run out in August 1989, five years after Kemper paid the last installment of the settlement money to Mitch? Or had the clock not started ticking because the fraud scheme continued as long as Phil led a double life?

"The U.S. Attorney at Seattle decided in early 1993 not to explore any further mail fraud prosecution," explained Jim Bordenet, U.S. postal inspector and public information officer of the Seattle Division, "because they determined that the statute of limitations had indeed run out."

While the court docket didn't include a mail fraud arrest or conviction, postal inspectors made substantive contributions to the investigation.

"Only an arcane vagary of the law protected Champagne from standing before the bar of justice on a postal violation," commented Bordenet, "perhaps the only bar that Phillip wasn't interested in visiting."

From behind bars at Spokane's Geiger Corrections Center, Phil, via the United States Postal Service, sent Mitch Champagne an "I know I owe you an explanation, so here goes" letter.

"When I fell overboard I somehow survived. I don't know how. I remember nothing for three or four days. ... I hope one day to go into detail in person if you are speaking to me. According to the paper, they say there was a $1.5 million fraud. I knew of some insurance, but nothing like that. ... I hope I have not caused you so much hell that you will wish I was dead. I love you."

He also wrote Gary Penar a combination thank you and entreaty for assistance letter.

"Without your expertise, I know I would have received a more severe sentence," acknowledged Champagne. "Knowing you were on my side gave me hope and kept me sane during the darkest hour of my life."

The hours were still pretty dim. Phil begged Penar to convince prison caseworker Ray Garcia that Phil was not Ronald Kollister, which was an identification error that continued to plague him. Despite confirmation from the United States government that Phil was not Ron, the judge took Kolliser's arrest record into consideration when sentencing Champagne.

"To compound the problem and make matters worse, they are certain that I am a drug user because of the pre-sentence investigation report," wrote Phil from prison. "Is there any way that you can possibly make him understand the report is in error?"

In light of Phil Champagne's history of fabricated names and bogus identification, the closing request resonated with irony: "I very much appreciate any help you can give me in setting the record straight as to my true identity."

Unlike elder brother Mitch, little brother John Robin never received mail from Phil.

"My first reaction, when it was confirmed that Phil was alive, was to go see him," said John, "But I didn't know if he wanted to see me. After all, in all those years, and even after he was discovered, he didn't call me or write me. I thought—and I know this sounds crazy—I thought that maybe he was mad at me for not saving his life when he fell off the boat. I got the name of the place where they had him from Mitch, and then I called and asked what I had to do to come visit him. They said he would have to put me on the visitor's list. I asked if they would see if he would do that."

Phil put John on the list.

"I figured then that he really did want to see me, so I went to Geiger, walked through the little turnstile, and there was Phil looking just like himself, and he looked pretty good."

There was no question as to whether John would hug him or slug him.

"I hugged him and held on a long, long time."

Daughter Renee and her husband, Steve Harold, also went on a pilgrimage to Geiger. For the first time in more than ten years, for the first time since his watery demise, Renee gazed upon the face of her beloved father. Everyone cried.

Kathy, Curtis, and Phil Jr., did not ask to be put on the list.

"In time I hope they will come around," said Phil. "It is hard for me, too. I am the same man who raised them from childhood, but in some ways I'm not the same man they knew."

John Robin immediately noticed alterations in Phil's character and demeanor.

"It was hard talking to him, because I could feel the influence living in prison was having on his mind. Some parts of him were the same as before; other parts were different. His faith in himself and his confidence were almost completely eroded. He was always the kind of person who could pretty much do whatever he decided to do. If he didn't know how to do something, he would learn how to do it. He has an extremely good mind and a great deal of perseverance. He can learn how to do anything he needs to do. It used to be that he used that talent to make money."

He used that talent to make money in an Idaho shed.

"Phil was always the eternal optimist," asserted Don Robertson. "He always believed that the next project was the one that was going to really make him money. Phil has a lot of talent, and I know he wants to make something of his life.

So did Montel Williams.

"Who is Montel Williams?" asked Phil as he went through his mail at Geiger.

Montel Williams, a former military man who's made his living for years as a television talk-show host, wanted to base an episode of his program around Phil Champagne. He thought it was an incredible story worthy of extensive TV coverage. Williams wanted Phil, wanted an exclusive, and wanted it for free.

Inside Edition and *A Current Affair* pursued Phil, Barb, Phil's kids, Lyle Workman, Tim Ohms, Henry Kantor, and Peter Richter.

"Yumpin' Yesus," chuckled Phil, "I think I need an agent."

What he really needed was to make peace with himself, his family, and Barbara Ellen LeHew Yokum Fraley Stegeman Champagne. Both Phil and Barb were locked up in the same facility.

"We didn't get much time together, and none of it alone," said Barb, "and even though we were married, I didn't know how much of what he said to me about anything was true. After all, I didn't know he had an ex-wife and kids until I read it in the paper."

Phil could top that.

"I didn't know I was dead until I read it in the paper," he said. "All things considered, I took it rather well."

EPILOGUE

As subjects, we all live in suspense, from day to day, from hour to hour in other words, we are the hero of our own story. We cannot believe that it is finished, that we are "finished," even though we may be so; we expect another caper, another installment, tomorrow or next week.

--*Mary McCarthy*
On the Contrary

Barb saw freedom earlier than Phil. Released from Geiger, she faced the toughest time of her life.

"No matter how hard things had been in the past, the situation after I was released was the roughest of all," confirmed Barb. "Our living conditions were poor, I was poorer, and Phil was still at Geiger."

On February 22, 1994, Phillip Wendell Champagne was a free man. To celebrate, he and Barb drove to Portland for a good buddy reunion with Ed Grass, Don Robertson, and John Robin. A splendid time was had by all. Mitch, still being hounded by the relentless Peter Richter, did not join his brothers for a backslapping evening of camaraderie and vodka.

"I am happy to inform you that Federal Kemper has dismissed their suit against my client, Mr. Mitch Champagne," announced a jubilant Henry Kantor in September 1994. "I am not at liberty to reveal the details of the settlement, but I can tell you that an amicable agreement has been reached; the suit has been dismissed."

Kantor's opponent, Peter Richter, was equally pleased to have the strange case of Phil Champagne finally resolved.

"I spent twelve years on that one," laughed Richter, "and now I'm on to a new one. Besides, I think Federal Kemper was getting tired of the whole thing anyway."

Life goes on in fair imitation of normalcy. Barb works in a restaurant; Phil picks up small jobs here and there and considers going on those television talk shows after all. Hollywood toys with some movie ideas, but you never know. Few folks outside show business feel comfortable hiring a high-profile felon.

"If you can't trust a man convicted of bank fraud and counterfeiting," joked the former Harold Stegeman, "who can you trust?"

Richard Fraley, Barb's first husband, drove from Shelton's Washington Corrections Center across the state and over the border into Idaho for the single purpose of making amends.

"I wanted to apologize for not being a better husband and father," admitted Richard. "Maybe things would have been different for Barb and the kids if I had been there for them more. I wish Barb and Phil all the best. I know it is not going to be easy."

In a comfortable split-level house on a corner lot in a quiet suburb, Barb's grandchildren were playing on backyard swings, sucking on popsicles, and crawling all over Phil Champagne. His growls elicited giggles, much as did those of Marlon Brando in *The Godfather*'s final scenes.

Sitting at the kitchen table eating cookies and swapping stories, it is difficult to envision this delightful man in his mid-sixties crawling through the mud on his belly to retrieve bogus bills from a Ritzville phone booth, running from Cancun assassins, or skydiving into a drug lord's lair to liberate a banker's box of illicit loot.

"Alias Mike lives somewhere in Oregon, obscure and silent, hoping no one shows up looking for him or asking questions," explained Phil. "If they do, he'll deny everything. He kinda wishes I had kept my mouth shut about all that stuff. We don't talk since the counterfeiting business, and I haven't seen him since before Barb and I left Shelton. When I got arrested, that was the last straw as far as being close friends went. He saved my life, and when he gave it back to me, I screwed it up."

Phil examined his empty glass.

"I called Mitch the other day and asked him if he was still mad at me. I never wanted to cause him problems, and I wondered if he still felt that his problems were all my fault."

Champagne rearranged a few cookie crumbs on the table.

"There wasn't much said, except that I should just let it go, that he wasn't mad anymore, but..."

Champagne shrugged, looked wistfully out the window, and shifted the subject as he got up from the table to get fresh ice for another round of soft drinks.

"Years ago, Joanne, the kids, and I were visiting her mother, Florence LeGate. Someone is always supposed to take pictures when families get together, so I was taking pictures. I wanted Renee to sit on a ladder while I took her snapshot. I couldn't get her to smile. I kept telling her to smile, but the sun was in her eyes. I got so irked at her for not smiling that I raised my voice, and the poor little girl started to cry. God, I felt like such a stupid ass making my kid cry just to take her picture."

Champagne returned to the table, glass and cookie in hand. He sat down, still talking about his kids as if they were not adults who, for the most part, wanted little or nothing to do with him.

"My son, Curtis, was born with what they call a lazy eye. He had to have them operated on when he was about four. His mother didn't get into these things, so I had to take him to the doctor and the hospital and decide if he needed the operation. They operated on his eyes, doing something to the muscles."

Champagne stopped, laughed self-consciously, and dabbed at his own eyes with a convenience-store napkin.

"He was in his bed when I got there and his eyes were bandaged but one of the bandages had come loose. I got mad and gave the nurse hell. The whole time Curtis had been lying there, waiting, and he couldn't see. And then I heard a little voice say, 'Daddy? Is that you?'"

As if his post-death adventures and Curtis's eye operation were inseparable events, Phil Champagne finished the story.

"I had always thought I would come back to life sooner or later, although I couldn't see how it would happen. Then again, were it not for the counterfeiting, I could have lived out my life as Harold Stegeman and gone to my grave without anyone ever knowing I had once been Phil Champagne."

Phil's critical thinking abilities had not changed much since second grade. And, for the record, he was not sorry that he'd run away from home.

"Had I not gone for it when I had the chance, I never would have experienced a decade of adventure, romance, danger, wealth, and what they call living under the shadow of the sword, and I would never have met Barb. Through everything, she loved me. She still loves me, and that's worth more than all the real money and fake money put together."

Lyle Workman has retired from the Secret Service. His big adventure was watching his son play basketball for Pepperdine University.

Assistant U.S. Prosecutor Timothy Ohms has matured into a respected professional who no longer frets about his future while sipping holiday eggnog.

The former site of Barb's Country Kitchen and Stegey's Blue Room is, at last report, vacant and available.

Extensive remodeling has beautified Perkins Restaurant in Ritzville, Washington. Linda Bright is still there serving up breakfasts and making change at the cash register. No hundreds, please.

AFTERWORD BY PHIL CHAMPAGNE

When the book came out, and the local newspaper ran a big story about me complete with full color picture of my smiling face, a woman stopped me on the street. She recognized me from the newspaper story, and launched into a tirade about what an awful person I was.

The woman spewed forth every insult you can imagine, and perhaps a few you can't imagine. I just stood there and let her go for it. Eventually, she ran out of both insults and breath. My response? Simple. I just looked at her with warmth and sympathy as I said:

"I bet your husband wishes he could fall off a sailboat, too."

A few years ago I applied for a passport so that I could go to Mexico to see my brother, John Robin. That's when the fun began. The first thing they ask is "Have you ever had a passport in another name?" As you know, I had a fraudulently obtained passport under the name Harold Stegeman. Suddenly, they got very excited. They wanted school records, job records, driver's licenses and much more going back to birth. I sent them what they asked for, but it was never enough. They kept asking if I wanted to withdraw by application for a passport.

Mitch ended up getting involved because it was pissing him off. He and his new wife were going with us to Mexico. So he hired an attorney to write a letter reminding them that I served my time, and the fact that I was once known as Harold Stegeman was irrelevant. There was no reason for them not to comply with my passport application. He was correct, of course, and they finally gave me a passport in my real name, Phil Champagne. We had a wonderful time, and no one was trying to kill me.

Use this link to sign up for advance notice
of new books from Burl Barer:
http://wildbluepress.com/AdvanceNotice

PICTURES

The Champagne Brothers
Mitch, John-Robin, Phil

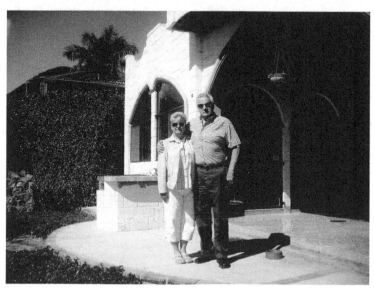

Phil Champagne and Barb Fraley

Phil Champagne

Phil with Las Vegas showgirls

Phil's fake Cayman Island driver's license as Harold Stegeman

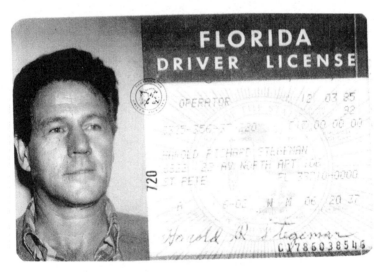

Phil's fake Florida driver's license as Harold Stegeman

Secret Service Special Agent Lyle Workman

Mug shot of Barb Fraley taken after her arrest at Perkins Pancake House.

The identification montage criticized during Fraley's trial.

Mugshot of Barb Fraley and montage of "female suspect"

Retain
Tim Ohms

Prosecuting Attorney

■ **Responsive to Asotin County**

"Tim Ohms has performed the duties of Asotin County Prosecuting Attorney in a very complete & professional manner. Mr. Ohms' full-time commitment to the Prosecuting Attorney's office has been a tremendous asset to Asotin County."

—Harley Williams, Chairman
Asotin County Board of Commissioners

■ **Responsive to Law Enforcement**

"Tim is refreshing. It's the first time we've had a full-time prosecuting attorney unrestricted by private practice. Tim is responsive—always willing to discuss points of a case, new policies or changes to upgrade the county."

—from an interview with
Sheriff Don Steele, August 1988

■ **Experienced**

The Prosecutor has a unique role as the legal advisor for the county. Tim has over two years' experience in the Asotin County Prosecuting Attorney's Office, and has served as Prosecuting Attorney since January, 1988.

■ **Dedicated**

Tim is the first full-time prosecuting attorney since 1978.

— Democrat —

Paid for by Committee to Retain Tim Ohms, Prosecuting Attorney

Election campaign flyer for Tim Ohms.

BONUS PAGES

RECORDING OF INTERVIEW WITH PHILLIP CHAMPAGNE ON JUNE 1, 1992, UNDER FILE NUMBER 410-711-15992-6. PRESENT FOR THIS INTERVIEW IS MR. CHAMPAGNE'S ATTORNEY, GARY PENAR, AND SA LYLE WORKMAN WHO WILL BE CONDUCTING THE QUESTIONS.

WORKMAN: The purpose of this interview is to put down the facts as Mr. Champagne recalls them concerning his initial decision to counterfeit money, in this particular case C-15902 and C-15992 *Notes*. To continue with the interview of Mr. Champagne concerning this explanation of the counterfeit activities covering the period roughly from October 1991 to March 1992, it is understood by the three of us involved with this statement that any deviations to this statement concerning violations outside counterfeiting activities are unintentional and will be stricken from the final written statement by agreement with all parties.

WORKMAN: Mr. Champagne if you could start by looking at the outline that we have generally prepared to cover this period of time, could you explain the why's and whim's of how you began to think about counterfeiting.

CHAMPAGNE: I first thought about it in early 1991.

WORKMAN: Early? January, February?

CHAMPAGNE: No.

WORKMAN: June or July?

CHAMPAGNE: Probably, yea, it could be as early as January or February, March. I don't remember exactly. Just the idea came to my mind for some reason or another and I decided to pursue it. It's something that I had years ago thought about, talked about, ya know, and discussed with people, I don't even remember who or how far it went, but I remember looking into it at that time. I don't know if there was a lithographic process at that time or not. But then the only thing I heard about was etching metal with acid, and I gave the whole idea up. I wasn't really in to it anyway; it was just talk more than anything else.

WORKMAN: This was the idea years ago. Now when you thought about it, you were thinking more along the lines, ah, did you know anything about offset printing then or did you have to actually do some studying before you got into the purchasing of equipment or what have you?

CHAMPAGNE: I knew a little bit about offset from people that I had talked to that I realized it was printed onto a rubber pad and then it was printed off again, and that's why it was called an offset press. But I just heard that.

WORKMAN: You've never been employed as a printer in your life?

CHAMPAGNE: No. We didn't even know what a press looked like. Anyway, I went and researched it as best I could at the time and just read books on it. It told you that you could buy plates that were ready to process and put them on the press and the press did the rest.

WORKMAN: Did you go to a local library? Where was your source of reading material? Just out of curiosity.

CHAMPAGNE: Local library.

WORKMAN: Coeur d'Alene? Spokane?

CHAMPAGNE: Coeur d'Alene Library.

WORKMAN: OK.

CHAMPAGNE: I think I read a book called "The History of Photography" and then another one that's "Modern Offset Press."

WORKMAN: When you were doing this studying on counterfeiting, is this while you were living at W. 1123 Hayden Ave.?

CHAMPAGNE: Yes.

WORKMAN: In Coeur d'Alene, or Hayden Lake, rather?

CHAMPAGNE: Yea, it's Hayden.

WORKMAN: Had you mentioned this idea to anybody else, specifically Barbara Fraley, at that time?

CHAMPAGNE: No.

WORKMAN: Richard Fraley?

CHAMPAGNE: No. No one. I just kept it to myself because I really didn't think it was possible, but I looked into it.

WORKMAN: What was your first step then?

CHAMPAGNE: I, ah, it's going to be difficult to remember it all, but I called some supply places in Spokane and asked them about the availability of lithographic plates, developers and whether they were sold to the public or you had to be a printer. I was informed they didn't--they could sell it to anyone, it didn't matter. Generally, they just sold to printers, of course. It was about that time, again I'm not sure of the date, that I talked to a printer. I just picked him out of the phone book. He was in Hayden on Commercial Ave. I forget the name of the outfit. His first name, if I remember right, is Chris. I talked to him on the phone to see if I could buy some plates from him, just for

experimental purposes, 3-4 plates, because the suppliers told me
I'd have to buy them a hundred at a time or 50 or whatever it was.
I think it's a hundred at a time. I didn't want to buy that many.
I didn't have the money. So, he said, yea, he'd give them to me
for a dollar a piece or whatever it was, so I could experiment
with them. That's what I did.

WORKMAN: Did you mention. . . what was the reason that you wanted
to experiment with them? Why would a printer agree to do this to
somebody who wasn't in the printing trade?

CHAMPAGNE: Right. I think before he asked I told him that I was
working on some type of greeting cards that I was going to do a
special way that I was going to use this process in a special
fashion that an ordinary printer couldn't just do for me or it
would cost a lot of money. Anyway, he seemed to think that that
was reasonable and he gave me other advice. I don't remember what
it was at the time. I think I asked him if rather than using arc
lights, well, I asked him about the plates. I said "Do you use an
arc light if you do your own plates?" He said "yes, I do." In
the conversation it came out that any kind of an ultraviolet light
would act on the material on the plate. Because, ah, you know, I
wanted to get by cheap on this. So, ah, I, ah,

WORKMAN: You drove to his shop and got the plates.

CHAMPAGNE: I drove to his shop and I got that stuff, and I did
some experimenting by putting something on the plate. I cut a
piece of the plate off with scissors and saved the rest of it and
put it back in the box. I put a little piece of something on
there, a piece of paper, and turned the light on it and developed
it to see if it would leave it where the light baked it on. And,
it did. A real sharp image. So I could see that that would work.
Then I realized that I would need a negative, actual size negative
of a bill. There again, a copy camera was out of the question.
So I went to St. Vincent DePaul and bought several Polaroid
cameras and other cameras.

WORKMAN: Spokane St.?

CHAMPAGNE: Coeur d'Alene. They had a whole box full of cameras
and I took the lenses off of some of them and bought the Polaroid
lenses. I made a box out of wood, waferboard as a matter of fact,
approximately 1-ft. square. Drove a hole in it, an inch hole, and
held the lenses off, took the front of the camera off, held the
lens up to it and looked through it to see if I could get any kind
of an image that wasn't totally blurred. The one that turned out
to be the best was the Polaroid camera. I then took screws,
screwed it on over the hole, caulked around it, had a hell of a
time getting it tight to stay there, and then by putting lights on
the other side of it and looking through, I realized I had to have
something to cast the image on. I don't know where I got the

information to use frosted glass. Some place in one of my conversations with someone, they said to use frosted glass like an old portrait camera. You just hook on and there's the image. Upside down and all that sort of thing. So, I didn't have any frosted glass. I shopped around and called around to try to find frosted glass. Couldn't find any. So I ended up taking a piece of plain glass and scotch tape and put strips across and held it up and there was my image. Surprising as it might seem, it worked very good. I built a frame and set that up on a frame. Then there was too much light around it. So I ended up taking waferboard again. I built a box about 4 ft. x 4 ft., 6 feet tall. Built it in the corner of the shed there at the same address. Made a door on it and sealed it with caulking and got inside and closed the door and turned the lights on outside and looked for light leaks and fixed them until I got them all. Had the door pulled shut and put rubber weather stripping in it to pull it shut to make it light tight. I found out later it wasn't necessary to be that light tight because the film was so slow it didn't affect it that much. Anyway, there was a bench I pulled it up outside, I put a board up, I put a bill (I think it was a $1 bill) and adjusted it back and forth and looked inside and adjusted that back and forth and I got a very sharp image. Right away I could see that that would work. I found another lens there that worked pretty well too but it distorted it. It made a dip in the center, curved the lines on it, so somebody told me along the line that that had to do with focal length. I don't know anything about focal length, but I guess they were right. So I put that lens in, I drove a hole through the wall and put a wire through. The lens that I had was the automatic lens from _____ the batteries. They had a little electric eye on them. I put black tape over the electric eye and hooked batteries up to it. I took it or cut the thing right off the camera. And then I pushed this wire through which went down the front of the camera and when I'd shut the shutter, it would go "click." As long as it couldn't get light, it wouldn't shut off; it would stay open. Then I turned it to its largest opening so I could get the image on there and that's how I got the image. Then because on the directions on the film it said f22 @ 15 seconds with 2,000 watts light or whatever it was, I didn't know what f22 was but I knew it wasn't a great big opening, so I imagined it was smaller. So I ran it down to the smallest opening, and I bought Inland Photo Supply, bought 4 500-watt photo floods. It called for some other light, but I couldn't afford them. So I got these bulbs and tried it. Got my image on there, closed it down. Then I bought developer. I mixed my developer and had a little temperature trouble but it didn't seem to bother too much. I made a shelf behind me and I put my developer, stop bath and fix and had a safe light up in the corner. I turned the lights on and got in there. I made a switch so I could turn the lights on and off from the inside. I got in there, closed it up, turned the lights out, took my film out, slid it in front, I had two rubber bands in front of the frosted glass, put it down in front. Bang, bing goes the camera _____.

When the shutter went, I could see the image. Then I counted off 15 seconds which was suggested in the brochure with the film. The very first one came very, very close. As soon as I closed that off, it was dark again. I took it and developed it. Put it in the fix. I kept it in the fix for a full 5 minutes before I even turned my safe light on. I discovered if I could turn the safe light on immediately it didn't hurt a thing. All kinds of things. Anyway, I took it out and held it up to the light and it was a very good, clear, sharp image, slightly faded on the outer edges. I discovered by moving the light in different positions, I got a good negative.

WORKMAN: When did you decide what denomination and where did you get the pattern note, the original $100, to make your first negative of the product that we know now as the end results?

CHAMPAGNE: I don't know when I made the decision to go with $100's because as one time I did all different sizes. They weren't complete.

WORKMAN: Can you remember what thought you gave to the $100 FRN that you chose to be a pattern note? Was there any great thought put into the series, the type or anything else?

CHAMPAGNE: No. None whatever. I just, ah, in fact, the matter is that particular bill was in the possession of one Monte LeHew. He happened to have it with him at a coffee shop and I saw it. It looked like a new bill. I asked him if I could borrow it for a day or two.

WORKMAN: Monte LeHew?

CHAMPAGNE: Yea, that's Monte LeHew, Sr.'s son.

WORKMAN: Can you spell that name? Is it Le . . capital something?

CHAMPAGNE: Yea, L-E, capital H-E-W.

WORKMAN: And the significance of -- who is he in relation to you or isn't he?

CHAMPAGNE: He's my wife, Barbara's, brother's child. I happened to spot it on him and I didn't think that they'd think anything of me borrowing $100 from him. Anyway, he just agreed to let me have it. I had it for 2-3 days, and I photographed it. It was a fairly new bill and that was the only reason I selected it.

WORKMAN: Was that bill on the . . . was the Federal Reserve Bank a New York Federal Reserve Bank on the pattern note? Do you understand what I'm asking? Did you change the . . . how did you decide to use the New York Federal Reserve Bank seal which is the second . . . you were telling me earlier, if I'm not mistaken, that didn't you change a San Francisco Reserve note by eliminating the 12 making it a 2 eliminating the 1? Can you explain that to me again.

CHAMPAGNE: Yes, I didn't do that on the first batch. I just used it as it was and then later when I made some more, I was trying to improve them. I didn't want to use the same serial number or even the same mint so it wouldn't be easily spotted. If I remember right, I took a number off a $1 bill and to protect a $1 bill I had started with a B, the number started with a B, so I had to match that. I just cut that seal out and replaced it with the other seal and blacked out the 1 to make it a 2. So, that explains that. The only reason I did it is because . . .

WORKMAN: That was your method of changing the serial numbers . .

CHAMPAGNE: Right.

WORKMAN: And, ah, I see, so one of the other notes you actually used as a pattern note was probably San Francisco Reserve Bank note with the numerical 12's in the four inner corners and it had the L black seal, you replaced that with the B from the first note that you worked with.

CHAMPAGNE: Right.

WORKMAN: How much time did you spend trying to, or do you agree that your original negatives needed to be touched up from, and/or any changes made to them, and what did you do in the process?

CHAMPAGNE: They had to be changed because I had to separate the seal which is green from the black word "100" stamped through it. The way I did that was I took the, I forget what you call it, it's a black material, I took it on a toothpick and I just blacked out the figure 100 stamped through the seal, leaving just the seal. Then I blacked out the serial numbers. Then I had just the face. Then on another one, I blacked out the seal and left the word "100" and cut that part out of the other negative and put the word "100" in it with little tiny pieces of black tape. That way I could burn that end over the top of the number and seal. I believe that's how I did that. I remember doing another process when I took a $1 bill and an exacto knife and I very carefully picked the ink off of the figure "100" stamped through the green seal, leaving just the green seal and then I photographed the green seal, cut it out, and put it on the plate with the serial numbers.

WORKMAN: But the fact that . . . or in your final product, the fact that it was a 1990 series and that original genuine denomination would have had a security fiber in there really did not even enter your mind? It was not an important thing, or you just didn't know?

CHAMPAGNE: It didn't enter my mind at all. I had no knowledge of it. I only found out later that there was such a thing by watching cases on TV of counterfeiting over in Spokane, that someone held them up to the light and explained it was there. That's my first knowledge of it.

WORKMAN: How about any attempts on your part to reproduce the red and blue security fibers. Were you aware of those?

CHAMPAGNE: I was aware of the red and blue threads in the paper, and I just ignored it. I didn't do anything.

WORKMAN: OK. Let's continue. Can you tell me as you began to get to the point of printing from your negative and plates, can you tell me where some of the various spots you bought your supplies from and your experience what you ran into when you tried to run your first impressions from your plates produced by the negatives you just explained?

CHAMPAGNE: I bought the plates, ink and developer, plate cleaner, roller cleaner and some paper from Paper Plus in Spokane. And the graphic arts film from Inland Photo Supply, also in Spokane, and the developer for that film from them and four 500-watt blue flood lights, from the same place. I took my negatives and put them on a plate, put a piece of glass over it, put a weight on the glass to hold it down tight so it would make a good connection to the plate, and I used a regular sun lamp and timer and experimented with it. Discovered that about 18 inches away for 4 minutes burned the image in pretty good. Then when I saw I had a good image, at that time I didn't have the serial number or seal removed. I just made one all black to see what it would do. In the meantime, I discovered that I couldn't print without a press because I took some of these and I inked them and tried. I didn't realize at that time that it was a balance of ink of water built up and once it was built up you maintained that and the fact that it was moving at a certain speed and all that you managed to print. I thought you make one and print one. It didn't work that way.

WORKMAN: And you actually tried to make one and print one off of your plate?

CHAMPAGNE: Yes. As a matter of fact, I took a 8-10" piece of plastic sewer pipe that smooth and round and I got a blanket for an offset press. Had a heck of a time getting them to sell me one because I couldn't tell them what size press. I just told them to give me any one and they couldn't understand it. But they finally did. I just pointed at a box and they gave it to me. I fastened that on there and by taking a water roller and wetting it and inking it, I finally built it up a little bit and I tried to pick

it up on the pad and it was obvious it wouldn't work so I gave it
up. That's when I almost gave the whole thing up until I, for
some reason I talked to the printer again that gave me advice at
first, and he happened to tell me he knew where there was a press
that I could get for $350. So I made arrangements and got that
press. He helped me load it. I took it over to my place and
unloaded it and he gave me a booklet with it. I read the booklet
on it and I just kept working it, fooling with it and inking it
and running different things through it, parts of bills and what
have you, until I could see it would indeed print.

WORKMAN: Do you remember the brand and model?

CHAMPAGNE: Yes, it was a Multi 1250 offset press. What year, I
don't know, but it was a pretty old one.

WORKMAN: This was the same printer that you had talked to at some
weeks or months prior whose first name you think is Chris?

CHAMPAGNE: Right.

WORKMAN: Even at this stage that we're at you want us to believe,
and you say it is the truth, that this printer did not know what
your intentions were.

CHAMPAGNE: No, I'm sure he had no idea.

WORKMAN: OK. Go ahead and continue.

CHAMPAGNE: Ah, let's see where was I here.

WORKMAN: You just explained that you spent some time becoming
familiar with the Multilith 1250. Could you explain to me why you
did not use this machine to its capabilities? In other words,
earlier before going into the tape, you explained to me that in
your final printing process, you decided to print one image per
8x11 sheet of paper. Explain to me why you did this and how?

CHAMPAGNE: Well, ah, the way I did it is I printed, I took a
plate, put the negative image on it that contained the serial
number and seal and I measured it from the edges from the ends so
I could try to get it in the same spot and ran those through. Now
I didn't want to try to line up five or six that I could get on
one plate. I lined up one and I had one ream of paper of 500
sheets. It cost me $18, and I didn't have much money. So, I ran
that through and they all came out pretty good. But I wasn't sure
yet that I could even line up the face and make it look right and
then I'd have the back to line up, and if I had four or five of
them on there, I'd have more trouble lining up the back. So I
simply want to run through, and I figure 500 sheets with a $100
bill on each one was a lot of money. So, when I discovered that I
could line 'em up pretty easy and I turned it over to do the back

-9-

side then I lost many sheets because when I tried to mix my green
ink, and I thought I had the right color, it looked fine until it
was printed and then being little tiny specs it changed the green.
Then I wasted those. I'd have to clean the press, go through the
process again, change the ink. When I finally got it, my 500 was
cut down to maybe 200 and then I had a line-up problem there.
Specifically, I was thinking of turning it over and it would be in
exactly the same spot but it turned to be in the same spot on the
other side. I didn't think of this until after I'd done it. So I
had a heck of a time lining it up. Almost had to start over
again. But I finally made another plate and changed its position
and I printed the backs and the backs didn't look very good. For
some reason the green didn't want to come out right. So, I ended
up on my first batch, with a handful. I didn't count them. But I
had less than half of the 500. Then I had to, because these
particular ones were on a yellow ivory colored paper, it wasn't
the color of money. It didn't feel, it was too thick too. I
tried different coloring processes. I couldn't find any. Finally
I tried water color and that worked a little bit but it was
awful powdery feeling when it dried. So I got some clothes dye
and I got a yellow and a black and I had to have something to
lighten it and they didn't have white clothes dye that I could
find. So I went to an arts store and I got a white powder, I
think it was water color type powder, and that way I mixed and
remixed and mixed again until I got a color that looked pretty
good. I painted it on a small brush and let it dry. The color
would change when it dries. I'd make another one. Finally I got
it so they dried and it was pretty near the same color. I let 'em
dry. Did the back side the same way and let it dry and then took
an exacto knife and straight edge and cut them out. I made a
cardboard pattern same size as a bill, held it on there and then I
cut 'em out. By the time . . .

WORKMAN: In other words, let me interrupt, you cut out one
complete image from one 8x11 piece of paper?

CHAMPAGNE: That's right. I didn't have many of them left after I
went through this coloring process, but then I knew how to color
so the next time I wouldn't lose so many. Anyway, I ended up with
those few and they looked bad to me and I was about ready to throw
out the whole idea. Because I knew there was a flaw in them.
Anyway, at that point, I showed 'em to my wife Barb. She said "My
God, those look good to me. I can cash them and we need the money
really bad."

WORKMAN: Is she the only one that saw them at that point?

CHAMPAGNE: Yes.

WORKMAN: Other than yourself?

CHAMPAGNE: Only one.

WORKMAN: And you think, ah, this would, we're now talking close to October of 1991?

CHAMPAGNE: Yes, right in there somewhere. I'm not sure of the dates, but it must have been around October.

WORKMAN: Mr. Champagne, you were just talking about completing printing at least one side of the $100 FRN's you had been making and you showed these to your wife Barbara who thought they were deceptive. Can you continue on? How long was it before you completed the back sides? How many did you produce and then take me into how you decided to pass these bills and where?

CHAMPAGNE: Ok. I showed them to Barb. She thought that they were usable bills so I thought, I'm not sure now, but I think that I only had the front at that time. I went ahead and did the backs and after I fooled around and got the right color and everything as near as I could. She said the backs aren't as good as the front but who looks at the back. So, I said I was going to go ahead and print a few with the paper I had left and we had different types of paper which all got used up. Then I printed up the ones that I was going to keep and colored them. Burned everything else. Then I cut out the ones I was going to keep. Burned the left-over papers and the ones that were screwed up being cut out.

WORKMAN: Was that a routine of yours, to burn whenever you had completed, did you do the same with your negative attempts and what have you?

CHAMPAGNE: Yes. I burned as I went. There was a regular wood barrel in there in the shop. I burned as I went. When I got these colored as near as I could, I cut them out, ah, I'm trying to remember now. Anyway, I must have had about 70-80 of those. I'm not sure of that. Barb decided she wanted to cash them. I said fine with me if you think you can get away with it. I'll drive you around.

WORKMAN: How did you decide where you wanted to go? Now I know this to be fact that on October 15th, 1991 from sometime later in the afternoon of that date until the last known pass that I'm aware of until approximately 9 PM that that was the first day these bills were ever passed in this country. Is that correct? Secondly, can you take me through, how did you decide to pass them all in Spokane and can you remember as many as possible of the victims of those bills?

CHAMPAGNE: That's true. It was on that date, as near as I can remember. I didn't look or pay any attention, but I know now that that was indeed the date. Somewhere around 4-5:00 in the afternoon, we just decided to go to Spokane because Spokane's a larger place, drove in there, came down Sprague heading west on

Spraque and stopped at the first business that looked like they
could handle it or would and they took it and we just went right
down the line. I remember hitting fast food places, a pie place,
ah,

WORKMAN: Who was passing the money? Was it you and Barbara or
was it just Barbara?

CHAMPAGNE: Just Barbara. I was driving only. I didn't think it
looked good enough to pass as a matter of fact. But she did it.
I don't remember the names of the places. I could see them and
say, yea, we cashed one there. She was turned down one at one
place because of the serial number he said was already on a list
of bad ones or something like that, but he wouldn't do it. We
went down Spraque and eventually turned and went out Division
hitting fast food stores and another pie place on Division.

WORKMAN: Heading north on Division, you're talking about?

CHAMPAGNE: Yea, heading north on Division. And a lot of fast
food places and markets.

WORKMAN: What did you do with the different items that you
bought?

CHAMPAGNE: Took 'em home.

WORKMAN: All the pies. You just them all in the back of the van
. . .

CHAMPAGNE: Yea, put them in the back and that was it.

WORKMAN: How many do you think you passed in that one day?

CHAMPAGNE: We cashed 21, I'm almost positive it was 21. It could
have been 22. But I think it was 21 because it was a new thing to
us and we were keeping pretty close track. That was it. We went
back to the house. It scared me. I think it scared her, too, but
it scared me so I gathered up the rest of those bills. I'm trying
to remember as I go and make sure I get this right. I gathered up
the rest of them and I destroyed them all.

WORKMAN: So you then destroyed approximately 50-60 if you had
passed 20 or so, you ended up burning 50-60 $100's.

CHAMPAGNE: Right. I probably burned more than that because it
seems to me I had some I had not cut out yet that were saved
because they might have been usable. I burned those also. I'm
not sure if I burned all the negatives or used some of them again.
I can't remember if I burned them all and made new ones or what.
Anyway, that took care of that batch right there. I think that
anyway I just said if you want to cash some more of those it's

fine but I'm going to have to make them better than the ones we've got now.

WORKMAN: You were not satisfied with those?

CHAMPAGNE: I thought they were terrible myself, especially the back.

WORKMAN: As far as you can remember from that date which was October 15th, the next significant date we're coming up to would be November 6th and that's the date Barbara was arrested for passing the one at Perkins Restaurant in Ritzville. Do you recall any other days that you and Barbara passed any other money? Exclude we know we're coming up to the day before you went to Ritzville. I'm saying did you make any and pass several days after October 15th, or to your knowledge did anybody else have any of the money of the first batch?

CHAMPAGNE: Yes, when I made the second batch, I can't remember the serial number any more. I used to know the first 3-4 numbers and I could refer to it. I think that that's the one that had the B and I changed the serial number. Maybe I used the same bill, maybe the same negative on the face or not, but I made several others and I made several backs that appeared to be better than the other. Then I went over to the paper supply outfit in Spokane. It seems this time I went to an office supply outfit near the Paper Plus and I found some 100% cotton fiber bond, 20#, that had a better feel to it. I took that back and that's what I printed on. I think it had a watermark in it that disturbed me. Some of the bills were lost because they hit the watermark and I had to throw those out. So I lost a lot of paper there. I ended up with probably 70-80 bills again, after they were cut out and the bad ones were all burned or thrown away. Now, wait a minute. No, I had more. I had a whole bunch of them. Maybe 100 or 150 of them not cut out. So I must have ended up with more than I thought I ended up with and cut out, I had about 70-80. Because I took the ones that were still on the full sheet and put them in a cardboard box and put them under my bed.

WORKMAN: These are all the second variation?

CHAMPAGNE: Yea, these are all the second. The first is totally gone. Now I've got the second and I went with Barb. The date again I don't know, but it was prior to November 6th. I think November 6th is when the Ritzville incident occurred. Maybe two or three days prior to that. I'm not sure. I took Barb downtown Coeur d'Alene and she cashed 5-6 of these new bills. One of them was cashed at an auto parts place there, I can't think of the name of them, two of them were downtown in the new mall, one of them was at the liquor store. The others I don't remember. But there was only 5-6 cashed. One of them was turned down somewhere by a drug store, we cashed one in a drug store, and went next door and that was a hardware or something and they turned it down. I said that was enough. They don't look good enough to me and we were too close to home. So we quite at that time and went home. Then it was on the 6th of November that Barbara and her son Richard and myself left in Rich's car for the Seattle area. The exact destination unknown. We were just heading for an area that had a heavy business population in an attempt to cash some of the remaining bills which I had 60-70-75, I don't know.

WORKMAN: Does this mean to include Richard Fraley?

CHAMPAGNE: Ah, I'm not positive that he intended to cash any at that time but it is my belief that he probably would have.

WORKMAN: Do you feel that he was aware of what you and Barbara had done as far as passing and your manufacturing?

CHAMPAGNE: Yes.

WORKMAN: How long has he been aware of it? Is this a recent revelation to him?

CHAMPAGNE: Ah, fairly recent. I'd say he's been aware at that point in time only a few days.

WORKMAN: So he had no knowledge of the manufacturing and of the passing that you did with the first variation in Spokane, as far as you know?

CHAMPAGNE: No. He didn't. His mother may have told him or he may have gathered that something like that had been done. I'm not sure.

WORKMAN: Now, taking November 6th, can you take me generally through the events that happened to the best of your knowledge on that date? Did you plan as you were driving to Seattle in Richard Fraley's blue Subaru and with Barbara with intentions to go to Seattle to pass this money, when you stopped for breakfast at Perkins, tell me what were the intentions the best you knew and then what happened?

CHAMPAGNE: Well, as far as I knew, no one had any intentions of cashing any of the bad bills at Perkins or anywhere near there. We just simply stopped for breakfast. I knew that she had one on her, but I think that she took that, put it among the good ones just to have it done. It could have been done later; it could have been done sooner. She chose to do it then which makes me think that she planned all along to cash one there knowing I would object. Anyway, that's what happened. After breakfast, she got up and when I saw her reach in her wallet, I could tell what she was going to do and I protested but it didn't do any good. She was on her way. I'm still not sure if Rich knew at that time. I really don't know if he knew or not. I know he knew as soon as

something started to go wrong. So I saw what was going on and
went out to the phone and there was trouble.

WORKMAN: The phone booth you are talking about?

CHAMPAGNE: No, the phone in Perkins. I went to that phone at
first and tried to kind of stay away and as the time went on and I
could see that there was a lot of trouble coming up, I thought I
would just walk on over to the store. And that's what I said. I
opened the inside door and said "I'm going over to the store and
pick me up over there." Then I went over there and on the way
over I saw the phone booth down by the driveway and I went down
there and went in the phone booth so I could try to stay out of
sight and keep an eye on what was going on. The police came and
they were arrested and taken into custody and drove off. Well, I
knew I was in trouble because I had those bills that we were going
to pass in a brown paper sack in my lefthand blazer pocket. I
knew I couldn't go back to the car. So, I stepped out of the
booth, went down the ditch, put this sack under a big piece of
sod. I had some ID in my pocket that wasn't mine. I put it in
the phone book in the back of the phone book and then I left the
phone booth and went into the store. I knew they were going to
come back to get me as soon as they discovered there was a third
party. There wasn't any way for me to leave anyway. They came
back and got me and asked me if I had any counterfeit money on me.
I went through my wallet and everything and showed them that I
didn't. Then they took me down - asked me if I'd go down to the
police station. I said yes, and went down there. I asked them
what was wrong. They said that's your wife or whatever. I said
yea. They said well she cashed a counterfeit $100 bill. They
weren't sure at the time whether she was just a victim or she was
cashing the bills. They said they were going to hold us for the
Secret Service. I had no choice but to wait. I waited for the
Secret Service and they arrived some hour, couple of hours later,
and asked me to identify myself and fingerprinted and photographed
me. Rich and Barbara refused and they detained her and released
Rich and myself. They took me up to pay for the impound on the
car, Rich's Subaru. We came back and got that and drove away. I
wanted to go back to the phone booth and get the bad money I hid
there but I was afraid there was a trap. So, we went on back home
and with Rich's help I got the money I mentioned was under the bed
out, burned it, burned everything that I could think of burning,
and still there sat the press. I knew that any minute they'd be
there so I didn't want to be struggling it into the van. Because,
after all, having a press wasn't a crime. That was my thinking,
believe it or not.

WORKMAN: Let me interrupt you one second. So, you destroyed all
the money and all the negatives also? Any plates?

CHAMPAGNE: Everything. Took all the plates out that I had
discarded that I was going to do something with later that

wouldn't burn. I took them all out one at a time, put gasoline on them, took steel wool and scraped the images off, cut them up with scissors into little slivers, put them in a box. I took the inks, cleaners, developers, unused plates, and Rich and took them and hid them somewhere in the bushes. I don't even know exactly where. I know roughly where. He put them under some old building boards to try to keep it dry.

WORKMAN: Now this is at the Hayden Lake address?

CHAMPAGNE: Yes. Some place along the line there I took the darkroom down off the wall and cut it up in pieces and started burning it. I scrubbed the ink spots off the floor. I repainted the table, the big table I made that I was working on that had ink on it and cleaners and all kinds of things that could be chemically traced. I repainted it. When I was pretty it was as clean as I could make it, I hooked up the trailer which is a 28' Nomad with the van and I drove it up to Monte's place

WORKMAN: Monte LeHew?

CHAMPAGNE: Monte LeHew

WORKMAN: Which is in or outside of Sandpoint?

CHAMPAGNE: At that time, he lived in a rented trailer near Lake Cocolalla, north end, across from the store and tavern. That would put him on the west side of the highway. I parked the trailer behind that trailer with Monte's permission. Told him that I was in trouble. Told him what I'd done. He said he knew it anyway the minute I borrowed the $100 bill. He said it was ok to leave it there, that he didn't care. Then I got Danny, his other boy, and I think Rich went with me, I'm not sure, and went back and got the press. Put it in the van. Drove the van back out and hid them there. I stayed away for several days because I was sure that the Secret Service was coming to search and would seize me. I also knew at that point in time that they discover my true identity was not Harold Stegeman.

WORKMAN: Anybody else know of this at this time? The LeHew's or Barbara, did anybody know that your identity was different from what it was?

CHAMPAGNE: Yes. They did not know what, but I told them at that point in time that my real trouble was going to be, no matter if the evidence is all gone, they are still going to say this is not the right person. In a matter of three weeks, that was my estimate, they would come to get me. If not, just to question me, they sure as hell would want to know what the deal was. Because I didn't think there were any warrants out for me under my real name. So a few days later, maybe just the next day, I don't really remember. I drank some vodka there and kind of lost track of time. I was worried about the counterfeit money hidden by the phone booth because I knew someone would find it, turn it over to the Secret Service and they would immediately put two and two together and there was only one person in that phone booth with mud on his shoes and it was me. So, they would come to get me for that. So, I said "well, you guys drive me over there. I'm going to take a chance and try to get it. I think it's a trap. But, what the hell, they're going to find it anyway or they have already found it."

WORKMAN: "You guys" meaning Richard Fraley, Monte LeHew and Danny LeHew?

CHAMPAGNE: No. No. Monte LeHew didn't go. Just Danny LeHew and Richard Fraley drove me in Richard Fraley's Subaru. They stopped on the freeway, I jumped out and they sped away. I crawled through the grass, retrieved the money.

WORKMAN: At approximately what time of the day is this?

CHAMPAGNE: Must have been 3:30 in the morning.

WORKMAN: Several days after November 6th?

CHAMPAGNE: Yes. It was the morning of the third day, if my memory serves me. Then I saw that no one was there, no activity. They didn't grab me. So, I got up the nerve and went into the phone booth and retrieved the identification also. I don't even remember the name on it. I just threw it away. Cut it up and threw it away. I took the bills across the freeway, crawled back through the grass because I thought, you know, standing in that open country, if I just walked back over there, any deputy sheriff that came by and saw somebody at 3:30 in the morning walking along, I'd be stopped. So, I dropped back into the grass and crawled. I went across the freeway, put the sack of money by a post and looked it over real well so I could find it again. Then I walked back down through the underpass. At that point of time, it didn't bother me too much if I was stopped. I'd just say I got in an argument with me and they left me and went down there to have coffee, something like that. So anyway I walked down there to the next restaurant down from Perkins, that would be west of Perkins, and met them. We drove back by, picked up the money and went on back to Monte's place.

WORKMAN: Near Sandpoint.

CHAMPAGNE: Yea, near Sandpoint on Hiwy 53, whatever highway goes to Sandpoint, anyway. So, when I got out there, I have to admit that I drank vodka on the way back and I wasn't feeling any pain. So I took this out and I said I couldn't believe it was still there. It was soaking wet and a mess. I spread it out on the bed to dry. It covered the entire bed, so there still guess about 80

bills laying out there. Later on, I moved part of them off and
laid down on the bed and went to sleep. When I awoke, there were
a lot less bills. It's my belief that they were taken by Danny
LeHew, for sure, Rich Fraley, probably, old man LeHew, probably
his wife Pat, all grabbed some.

WORKMAN: Now, when you say old man LeHew, his first name would
be?

CHAMPAGNE: Monte. Monte LeHew, the father. I confronted them
with it. They all denied it. I said "Well, what happened to all
of them? There was more of them here." They said I burned some
of them because they were wet and torn. It's possible I did burn
some of them but not that many. I wasn't in that bad shape. I
knew that they had some. When it was dry, I bundled it up and
looked at it. It was salvageable. I almost threw it on the stove
right there but I didn't. I wrapped it up in plastic. Gave it to
Monte LeHew, the older Monte LeHew, and asked him to hide it for
me until I could come for it. He put it under the dog house.
Then took the press which is still in the back of the van, I drove
the van down to Coeur d'Alene, parked it on a side street to leave
it overnight until the mini-storage place was open. Then I went
and rented a mini-storage the next day. I stayed at 1123 W.
Hayden that night expecting to be arrested again any minute. Went
to the mini storage place which is Budget Mini Storage, I don't
remember the address. The mini storage was #113 a 5x10. I rented
it under the name of Wills, I think the first name was Larry but
I'm not sure. I told them I didn't have my driver's license with
me and that I'd bring the address later. I did and they were
satisfied with it. Rich went with me and helped me unload the
press and put it in mini storage along with some ink, the
cleaners, unused plates and I think that's about all that was
left. I left it there and paid three months' storage. I paid the
three months' storage in advance because I expected to be arrested
and that would give me three months at least grace before they'd
go in there and find out there was a press in the place. Maybe
then I thought I could call somebody and have them go get it out
of there for me, I don't know. Ah, so, that's where that ended
up. Then I went back and had more time to go through and destroy
anything that I thought might be evidence. Somehow I overlooked a
very important piece of evidence in my briefcase. I don't
remember how it got there. I must have had it with other scraps,
numbers that I had cut out to paste in and things like that, and
then when I cleaned it out to burn them, simply missed it. Now,
that pretty well takes me up to, ah. . .

WORKMAN: That's virtually the end of the first counterfeiting
with two variations.

CHAMPAGNE: That's where it ended, right there, yes.

WORKMAN: So, then the next we're going to talk about is you don't

think that anybody cares or you've gotten away with it or whatever
and we'll go into that in just a second (go to tape #2).

WORKMAN: The last place that we ended up on the last tape was you
had just put the press into the mini-storage and you were back to
your garage at W. 1123 Hayden Ave. doing the last cleanup of what
you considered would be evidence held against you. Now we want to
conclude with what you as previously explained as thoughts of
possibility continuing with the counterfeiting because for
whatever reason you were not certain that anybody was really aware
of your activity.

CHAMPAGNE: Well, see after destroying what I thought was the rest
of the evidence, or looking around the shed and the house for
evidence, I can't remember the exact date or how long after that
it was but it had been some months, and I had foolishly assumed at
that point in time that I was no longer under investigation and
that they had not evidentally sent in my fingerprints in the first
place and had only kept them for their own record. I didn't think
it would take that long to identify me. I thought the FBI could
do it in three weeks. So, foolishly, I decided for some reason I
guess because I was broke that I perhaps should set the press back
up and print some counterfeit money just to have in case I needed
it in the future. That doesn't sound too bright, but that was my
thinking on it. So, ah, of course I needed a place to do it and I
couldn't do it around the house. I looked around for a place to
rent. I found a place on Government Way. I don't remember the
address. There was a sign on it that says "Car Care." It was an
old shed, lefthand side going north, out quite a ways. I even
forget what I rented it for. Seems to me it was $180 a month, but
I'm not sure. It was in the paper and I called on it and talked
to a man. Don't remember his name. Rented it from him and gave
him the name Frank Wincheski. I also put the lights in the name
of Frank Wincheski. I think went, I don't remember the time that
passed on this but somewhere around the 1st, 2nd or 3rd of
January, I went to the mini-storage place where I had the press.
I disassembled the press into three or four parts so that I could
move it by myself. Moved it into the van along with the other
paraphernalia that was, some ink and plates and a few things like
that, and took them to the new place. Unloaded them and went and
got some particle board and made a dark room, made the camera,
took the lens and the camera and drilled some holes, put my safe
light in, and a few odds and ends like that. I don't really
remember how much more I had to do to finish. Somewhere around
the 10th or so, I'm not sure of the date on this, the 10th of
January, I saw someone I thought was following me. It frightened
me because I thought I was under surveillance from the Secret
Service, and I decided to end the operation once and for all right
there on the spot. I went back. Took the dark room down, sawed
it up into strips of wood, put it in the van, took it home and
used it for firewood. I contacted the printer that I had gotten
information from, Chris, in Hayden, and asked him if he knew

anyone who wanted to buy a press. He said he didn't but that he
would look around. I gave him my phone number. Three or four
days later he called me and said he'd buy it himself if I'd bring
it over. I went back and picked it up. Rich went with me. We
took it to him, the printer in Hayden on Commercial Ave. I
explained to him that I had disassembled it for the purposes of
moving it. I set it out on the sidewalk there. He had a man with
him. He introduced me but I don't remember his name that picked
the press up, buying it from Chris the printer. Chris gave me a
check for $300 for it. Said he would give me $150 but he wanted
me to take the $300 check to the bank and cash it and bring him
$150 back. I don't know why, but that's what I did. He ended up
with the press and that's where it is today.

WORKMAN: As far as you know, it is with the person who bought it
from Chris LNU, the printer.

CHAMPAGNE: That's right. I think he was a hobbyist, 60-65 years
old. The rest of the material there, the ink, and I cut the
plates up with scissors and put them in the trash at the Rathdrum
garbage dump off Hwy. 53. I left a note for the owner of the
building on the little bulletin board in the office saying that I
would no longer after January be there and left the keys hanging
and left.

WORKMAN: The only one who knew what your ideas were at this
point, or had been of possibly reprinting again, would have been
Richard Fraley?

CHAMPAGNE: Richard Fraley helped me move some things around so he
knew about it and Barbara also knew that I was doing something.
But I didn't tell her and we didn't discuss it except to say "I
need some money and it won't hurt to have this; I can always burn
it." She said she hoped I knew what I was doing. She said
"You're a damn fool." I have to agree that she was right at this
point. That pretty well covers it. No one else knew; the
LeHew's were not involved at that time, after them taking that
from me I didn't want them to know anything more.

WORKMAN: In reviewing what we've gone over on this portion of
this tape and the previous tape, let's list the people who now
know that you counterfeiting money and had at least seen it on one
occasion. Of course, that would be your wife Barbara, Richard
Fraley, Monte LeHew, his son Danny LeHew, and another son?

CHAMPAGNE: Yea, Monte

WORKMAN: Monte, Jr. LeHew?

CHAMPAGNE: Yea. And his wife.

WORKMAN: And his wife, Patricia or Pat.

CHAMPAGNE: Pat. I don't know whether it's Pat or Patricia. Those are the ones that I know of that know. But I'm sure that their friends know.

WORKMAN: You have reason to believe as you mentioned to me before that after you recovered the money that was in the paper sack from the phone booth in Ritzville, that that night as it was laid out on the bed in the home of LeHew that when you saw what you recalled in the amount of counterfeit that you had produced there was less there in the morning than what you thought there should have been and you accused . . .

CHAMPAGNE: Yea. There was definitely less there and I accused them of taking some.

WORKMAN: "They" being the LeHews in general?

CHAMPAGNE: Yes. All of the LeHews and Richard. It seems there was some friend of theirs or something there but I don't remember for sure. I don't think he was there at that time.

WORKMAN: They all denied it?

CHAMPAGNE: They all denied it, but I know for a fact that they did take it. I'm missing something here now. Oh, yes, when this money was dried out, I had Monte LeHew, the older Monte LeHew, the father, hide this under the dog house for me in a plastic bag. I later came back a day or so later, took it back from him and not trusting him any more, even then I think there was more gone at that time, but I couldn't tell you for sure. I took that package and went across the railroad tracks and hid it in the woods. Then I later came back and got that. Took it down to 1123 W. Hayden and hid it in a field out there because I was going to burn it but at the last minute decided to keep it and see what happens. That money was still there, ah, it's hard to remember this and get it in order, but that money was still there. I took it for some reason in the house. Evidentally, I had still figured I wasn't being watched and they weren't investigating me and it was about five months at that time. I took it back in the house and had it in a raisin box. I put the raisin box on a plastic container in a shelf on the porch to decide what I was going to do with it. For some reason, I didn't think I was in any danger at that time. I knew that I could burn it in a matter of minutes so I put it there. On the day I was arrested, I talked to Barbara before they took me away and whispered in her ear that it was there and to destroy it, and she assured me later on the phone that she had indeed burned it.

WORKMAN: That would have been the last contraband that you were aware of that was intact and that you had any control of or Barbara had any control of, ah. . .

CHAMPAGNE: That's right. And Barbara didn't know it was there. It was a complete surprise to her that I would be dumb enough to have it there. As it turned out, it didn't make any difference. I might as well have left it. But she went immediately and destroyed it.

WORKMAN: But you still have suspicions that of the second variation of your printing, which by the way we have concluded contained two separate serial numbers, and of this amount that was three nights after Barbara was arrested on the bed at the LeHew residence that some of this money was taken and you have suspicions to believe that they even passed it in the Sandpoint area.

CHAMPAGNE: I believed that they passed it or were instrumental in passing any and all of it that came out other than the one at Ritzville and the five or six that Barbara passed in Coeur d'Alene. They must have passed all of them.

WORKMAN: Other than money that you might have passed that an innocent person would carry on them we refer to as floating counterfeit, you and Barbara only passed your counterfeit money in Spokane on Oct. 15th and Coeur d'Alene on or about Nov. 3rd, 4th or 5th and in Ritzville on Nov. 6th?

CHAMPAGNE: That's . . .

WORKMAN: That is the extent of your passing of your own manufactured counterfeit money?

CHAMPAGNE: That is absolutely every bit of it. The rest was done by someone else. And I know who it was. I think it is the LeHews and Rich and/or their friends that they confided in to show "look here, I've got a handful of counterfeit money, ha, ha, ha, I'm a bigshot." That might be a friend of Rich's that lives in Spokane that I've since remembered was his girlfriend's friend that they mentioned from time to time. That's the only person I think they knew up there. Also, ah, . . .

WORKMAN: Any name to go with that memory?

CHAMPAGNE: No, no name at all. Old man LeHew. I got this second hand now, I didn't see it, so I don't know that it's true, old man LeHew, while in the Olympia area, talked to Rich in the Olympia area, and Rich told me this, and said "Here. . ." and gave him three $100 bills, counterfeit bills, back and said he had had ten but he had burned the other seven and he had found them in a book planted on him in his trailer near Sandpoint. Rich tells me he immediately burned the three bills. For what it's worth, if anybody wants to believe his story, I mean these are part of the ones that he stole and he was trying to cover himself.

WORKMAN: This would have been the second variation of what you manufactured?

CHAMPAGNE: Yes.

WORKMAN: At this time, I believe that we have initially covered everything that we agreed to cover and upon the completion of the transcribing of these tapes, will read them over and in agreement if they are true and correct to the best of your knowledge, will sign those and that concludes the information on this interview and tapes at this time.

United States District Court

_____ DISTRICT OF ___IDAHO_____

In the Matter of the Search of

(Name, address or brief description of person or property to be searched)
Stegeman residence and trailer located at W. 1123 Hayden Avenue, Hayden Lake, Idaho, described as a one story home, beige in color with brown trim, composite roof on south side, brown aluminum roof on north side, with a large tree in the center of the front yard (south side). Also, adjacent to the house in rear yard (north side) is a Nomad two wheel tandem trailer, beige in color with brown trimmed windows and with three stripes, brown, orange and beige, circling the trailer.

SEARCH WARRANT

CASE NUMBER: *92-3036 M-01*

TO: __United States Secret Service__ and any Authorized Officer of ~~the United States~~

Affidavit(s) having been made before me by ___Robert Kircher___ who has reason to
                                                            Affiant

believe that ☐ on the person of or ☒ on the premises known as (name, description and/or location) Stegeman residence
and trailer located at ~~W. 1123 Hayden Avenue~~, Hayden Lake, Idaho, described as a one story
home, beige in color with brown trim, composite roof on south side, brown aluminum roof on
north side, with a large tree in the center of the front yard (south side). Also, adjacent
to the house in rear yard (north side) is a Nomad two wheel tandem trailer, beige in color
with brown trimmed windows and with three stripes, brown, orange and beige, circling the
trailer.

in the_____ District of ___IDAHO___ there is now
concealed a certain person or property, namely (describe the person or property) United States Passport No. 041195289
in the name of Harold Richard Stegeman, other identification documents and related papers in
the Stegeman identity; and other identification documents and related papers in other
identities relating to the individual using the identity of Harold Richard Stegeman and
documents, related papers, bills and keys relating to the existence of alternate storage
areas where identification documents in the name of Harold Richard Stegeman, or another, may
be kept.

I am satisfied that the affidavit(s) and any recorded testimony establish probable cause to believe that the person
or property so described is now concealed on the person or premises above-described and establish grounds for
the issuance of this warrant.

YOU ARE HEREBY COMMANDED to search on or before ___March 13 ᵃᵐ/*₈*, 1992___
                                                                                        Date

(not to exceed 10 days) the person or place named above for the person or property specified, serving this warrant
and making the search (in the daytime — 6:00 A.M. to 10:00 P.M.) ~~(at any time in the day or night as I find reasonable cause has been established)~~ and if the person or property be found there to seize same, leaving a copy
of this warrant and receipt for the person or property taken, and prepare a written inventory of the person or prop-
erty seized and promptly return this warrant to __Magistrate Judge Stephen Ayers__
                                                                                                    U.S. Judge or Magistrate
as required by law.

___March 12, 1992 @ 10:23 a.m.___   at   ___Coeur d'Alene, Idaho___
Date and Time Issued   City and State

__Stephen Ayers__
__Magistrate Judge__   _[signature]_
Name and Title of Judicial Officer   Signature of Judicial Officer

AFFIDAVIT

I, Robert Kircher, being first duly sworn upon oath, hereby depose and say:

1. I am a Special Agent of the United States Department of State, Bureau of Diplomatic Security, assigned to the Seattle Resident office, Seattle, Washington. I have been a special agent with the Department of State since 1980. During the performance of my duties I have conducted investigations over the past 12 years in cases regarding false statements in making applications for United States Passports and know:

a. That persons that obtain passports under fraudulent or deceased identities have identification documents and related papers in their fraudulent identity. These identity documents and related papers are normally maintained where they are readily available.

b. That persons who are living under a false identity frequently have identification documents and related papers in their true identity and/or other fraudulent identities, and these items are normally kept in their residences or other locations which they maintain control over.

2. It is believed that a search of the above-described residence and trailer will reveal the United States Passport and other documents in a false identity which were used to obtain the passport in violation of 18 U.S.C. 1542, in the Middle District of Florida.

3. On March 3, 1992, I was contacted by United States Secret Service Special Agent Lyle Workman. He informed me he was doing an investigation on Harold Richard Stegeman, born 6/20/37 in Florida and had determined Stegeman was issued a United States Passport No. 041195289 on October 31, 1985. Special Agent Workman said his investigation has convinced him Stegeman was not who he claimed to be. He explained he could find no prior personal history on Stegeman until 1985, when Stegeman obtained a Cayman Island driver's license (5/12/85), a passport (10/31/85), a first time social security number (11/85), and a Florida driver's license (12/3/85).

4. I told Special Agent Workman that based on the fraud indicators he listed, an investigation would be conducted regarding a violation of passport laws.

5. On March 3, 1992, I called United States Department of State Special Agent Mike Hudspeth in the Miami Field Office. I requested he check with Florida Bureau of Vital Statistics and attempt to verify Stegeman's claimed date of birth. I requested he ask death records be searched for a record of death under Stegeman's name and date of birth. I also requested a copy of

...continued on next page

Stegeman's passport application and photograph from headquarters in Washington, D.C.

6. On March 3, 1992, Special Agent Mark Hipp, of my office, verified with the Seattle Passport Agency that Passport No. 041195289 was issued to Harold Richard Stegeman, born 6/20/37, in Miami, Florida, on October 31, 1985. The passport is valid until October 30, 1995.

7. On March 4, 1992, Special Agent Hudspeth called me and said Florida Bureau of Vital Statistics had verified Harold Richard Stegeman, born 6/20/37 in Florida, died November 4, 1945. This information was conveyed to United States Secret Service Special Agent Lyle Workman.

8. On March 9, 1992, Special Agent Hudspeth informed me a warrant had been issued on March 6, 1992, in the Middle District of Florida, charging the individual that obtained the passport under the Stegeman identity in violation of 18 U.S.C. 1542--False Statements in Application for Passport. Special Agent Hudspeth said Stegeman had been arrested by the United States Secret Service on March 6, 1992, on a conspiracy/counterfeiting charge.

9. On March 11, 1992, Secret Service agents that arrested Stegeman told me they had asked Stegeman if he had a United States passport and Stegeman replied he did. No passport was found upon Mr. Stegeman's person at the time of his arrest.

10. The person using the deceased identity of Harold Richard Stegeman lives at ████████████████████, Hayden Lake, Idaho. United States Secret Service Special Agents Lyle Workman and Milton B. Mikalson have observed Stegeman leaving that residence. On March 6, 1992, Stegeman was arrested by Secret Service agents. Stegeman stated his address was W. 1123 Hayden Avenue, Hayden Lake, Idaho.

Robert Kircher
ROBERT KIRCHER

ABOUT THE AUTHOR

Burl Barer, Edgar Award-winning author and two-time Anthony Award nominee, is a writer, producer, and director with extensive entertainment industry experience. Honored for his work in radio, print, and television, he is a frequent guest on TV series, including episodes of Investigation Discovery's *Deadly Sins, Deadly Women, Behind Mansion Walls, Scorned* and *Motives and Murders: Cracking the Case,* and the Oxygen network's *Snapped.*

Barer hosts the award-winning radio program "True Crime Uncensored" on Matt Alan's Outlaw Radio USA. Barer is also a contributor to Hart D. Fisher's "American Horrors." Channel on Filmon.com. He has also appeared on-screen in television productions and, in his words, "one minor motion picture." He is working on new adventures of Leslie Charteris' *The Saint,* as well as writing fact-based crime books and supernatural thrillers.

Other WildBlue Press Books by Burl Barer

Murder in the Family
http://wbp.bz/mitf

Headlock: A Jeff Reynolds Mystery
http://wbp.bz/headlock

With Frank C. Girardot, Jr

Betrayal in Blue
http://wbp.bz/bib

A Taste For Murder
http://wbp.bz/atasteformurder

See even more at:
http://wbp.bz/tc

More True Crime You'll Love From WildBlue Press

BOGEYMAN: He Was Every Parent's Nightmare by Steve Jackson *"A master class in true crime reporting. He writes with both muscle and heart."* (Gregg Olsen, New York Time bestselling author). A national true crime bestseller about the efforts of tenacious Texas lawmen to solve the cold case murders of three little girls and hold their killer accountable for his horrific crimes by New York Times bestselling author Steve Jackson. *"Absorbing and haunting!"*(Ron Franscell, national bestselling author and journalist)

wbp.bz/bogeyman

REPEAT OFFENDER by Bradley Nickell *"Best True Crime Book of 2015"* (Suspense Magazine) A "Sin City" cop recounts his efforts to catch one of the most prolific criminals to ever walk the neon-lit streets of Las Vegas. *"If you like mayhem, madness, and suspense, Repeat Offender is the book to read."*(Aphrodite Jones, New York Times bestselling author)

wbp.bz/ro

DADDY'S LITTLE SECRET by Denise Wallace *"An engrossing true story."* (John Ferak, bestselling author of Failure Of Justice, Body Of Proof, and Dixie's Last Stand) Daddy's Little Secret is the poignant true crime story about a daughter who, upon her father's murder, learns of his secret double-life. She had looked the other way about other hidden facets of his life - deadly secrets that could help his killer escape the death penalty, should she come forward.

wbp.bz/dls

BODY OF PROOF by John Ferak *"A superbly crafted tale of murder and mystery."*– (Jim Hollock, author of award-winning BORN TO LOSE) When Jessica O'Grady, a tall, starry-eyed Omaha co-ed, disappeared in May 2006, leaving behind only a blood-stained mattress, her "Mr. Right," Christopher Edwards, became the suspect. Forensic evidence gathered by CSI stalwart Dave Kofoed, a man driven to solve high-profile murders, was used to convict Edwards. But was the evidence tainted? A true crime thriller written by bestselling author and award-winning journalist John Ferak.

wbp.bz/bop